For many years, I have believed that Christians need to not just respond to what is happening in the public square, but actively get involved in the conversation. I'm grateful to Graham for sharing some helpful ideas and tips to help us start that journey, especially if this is new to us. This book provides an honest assessment of the landscape, speaking into the challenges we face but more importantly the many opportunities ahead to witness to Christ. I pray this book will help you, whether as a church leader or just a Christian to consider stepping up in making your voice heard in the public square.

ADAM MAY
Ministry Development Consultant and Public Relations Advisor

What I love most about this book is that it is immensely practical. Graham writes with a true pastor's heart. His longing to see sinners saved is combined with a passion to equip saints for mission. From wisdom on answering common objections to Christianity, to engaging the media and being salt and light online and in politics, this is an excellent call for Christians to combine truth and grace as we take the glorious gospel beyond just our own circles and into the public square. You'll find this book clear, compelling and creative.

JAMES MILDRED
Director of Communications and Engagement,
Christian Action Research and Engagement (CARE), Scotland

T0018288

REASONING
in the PUBLIC
SQUARE

Delivering the Changeless Message
Through Ever-Changing Media

Graham Nicholls

CHRISTIAN
FOCUS

Copyright © Graham Nicholls 2024

paperback ISBN 978-1-5271-1105-9
ebook ISBN 978-1-5271-1153-0

10 9 8 7 6 5 4 3 2 1

Published in 2024
by
Christian Focus Publications Ltd,
Geanies House, Fearn, Ross-shire,
IV20 1TW, Great Britain.

www.christianfocus.com

Cover design by
Daniel Van Straaten

Printed and bound by
Bell & Bain, Glasgow

Contents

Acknowledgments

Many have helped in the writing of this book including George Clayson (Open Air Mission), James Mildred (CARE), Jenny Taylor, Dia Moodley, Esther Higham, Joel and Josh and the Affinity Media Group, but a special thanks goes to Matthew Evans, and Dave and Sue Andrews for their patient editing of my challenging prose and to Christ Church Haywards Heath for allowing me some time and space to write.

Introduction
The Invisible Church

'You are the salt of the earth.
But if the salt loses its saltiness,
how can it be made salty again?
It is no longer good for anything,
except to be thrown out and trampled underfoot.'
(Matthew 5:13)

A burden for your marketplace

I have been a pastor in a medium-sized town in the UK for two decades. I know a lot of people. Some days I can walk down the high street and recognise nearly everyone. I can even remember some of their names.

On other days, I don't know anyone who shares the pavement with me, and they don't seem to know me. They also don't know my church or any church in the town (and there are plenty of churches – it's the Southern England Bible Belt here).

But much more important than whether they know me or the church is that so many of them don't know about Christ, and they are really not at all bothered about their ignorance. They don't even think they need to know; it has no relevance for them.

Most people are not interested in what is going on at our churches, however good the flyers, posters, and

1

promotional videos are. They don't think church is 'their thing', and anyway, they don't know, in any meaningful sense, anyone who is a member there. These are people you may not know at all, or you may just know them as regular faces on the street that you say hello to, but nothing more.

I see them walking by or driving past and I wonder how the gospel is ever going to reach them. What would make them look up with any curiosity or sense of need?

I wonder if you have ever had that experience? Have you ever felt a burden for the people in your town, city or country – those who will never get to hear about Jesus through their friends, families, neighbours and churches?

Think about all the voices they hear and all the images they see. How are they going to hear about the Saviour of the world?

They each have a worldview – and certainly not a Christian one – but they probably wouldn't recognise it as such even if you gave it a name and mentioned it to them. They are hopelessly lost, but most of the time they don't feel it.

They are just living their lives. They have jobs and families. They are worrying about their gardens, or how their kid is getting on in their new class or that medical procedure coming up, or about getting old. Some don't have a job and worry they will never get one. Some are worrying about their exams. They are thinking about that girl, or that boy, or the holiday they are planning. Maybe they've worked hard all week and want to completely get off their face tonight and have fun. Some are depressed and lonely.

They have their dreams but, at the same time, there is an anxiety about the future, but they are not looking to the church to give them answers. In the meantime, they would like to have enough money and enough love to get by comfortably.

How are we going to break through? What will attract their gaze?

How can we enter their marketplace – the places that people go, share life, goods and ideas?

Commissioned

In Matthew 28, when the risen Jesus was on His way back to the Father, He declared to His disciples that He has 'all authority in heaven and on earth' (v. 18). No one and nothing can stand in His way; He rules everywhere. He also promised that He would be always with them. Wherever they are, whatever day of the week it is, whoever they are talking to, He will be right there with them.

Then with that encouraging backdrop of the power and promise of Jesus, He says, 'Go' – make disciples and teach them. This command was not just for the original apostles, but for the church – all of us who have followed in their footsteps down the centuries.

In contrast to the Old Testament, when Gentiles (non-Jews) could experience the benefits of salvation only by journeying to Israel and the physical temple at Jerusalem, the spiritual, living temple of Christ's church now goes out to the Gentiles, meeting them where they are.

For the apostles, their mission started locally in Jerusalem and then moved outwards through Judea and Samaria, and from there to the entire Roman world. They began at the temple and the synagogues but ended up preaching anywhere and everywhere, to Gentiles as well as Jews. As the gospel message extended across the world, apostles such as Paul went to local marketplaces and lecture halls. He walked and talked beside the river where people gathered. He spoke in courtrooms and palaces. He went where the people were and where he could speak to them.

Good news to share

One of the core convictions of this book is that God has commanded all Christians throughout all the ages to share the gospel – a treasure entrusted to us that is to be passed on. It is both a privilege and a responsibility (1 Cor. 9:16-18). I am sure you feel it too.

We all want to share good news: The child that has just come first at sports day, slightly to our surprise; that exam we passed after all the hard work; the medical test that came back negative, to our great relief; the special offer voucher code, the programme we watched on Netflix and can't wait to share with other people.

We want to tell someone our good news.

If we are Christians, we believe the story of Jesus Christ – living, dying, and rising again – is the very best of good news. Good news that we want to share.

Most of us do share it when we can; maybe not often enough because we get lazy or fearful; maybe sometimes we falter and fail – we stumble over our words. But we know what we are *meant* to do and, on our best days, we do.

'Relational' evangelism – gospel conversations and invitations – should be the heartbeat of church outreach. Churches should encourage and complement this by putting on events, not for their own sake but as an enabler for evangelism, to give focus and motivation for our personal interactions with others, seeking to draw in those who might never otherwise engage with the church's community or its message.

So personal, relational evangelism is really important. But that is not, in the main, what this book is about!

Moving out

My passion in writing this book is that there are people we need to reach with the good news that we will never reach through our current family, work, and community connections.

We all have a role to play in sharing the gospel on the frontline (John 1:46, Eph. 4:11-13). And sometimes we need to find a new frontline. Why? Because we are not having much of an impact at the current one where we are engaged, the reason being that few people there are in the same 'place' as us.

The Office for National Statistics in the UK has published data from the 2021 census, showing that for the first time, less than half of the population in England and Wales – 27.5 million people (46.2 per cent) – described themselves as 'Christian'.[1]

According to the 'Talking Jesus' survey,[2] 'Practising Christians' (those who attend church monthly, pray and read the Bible weekly) make up about 6 per cent of the UK population. That means about 1 in every 17 people is a practising Christian. That sounds pretty good, doesn't it? Even if the figure is rather exaggerated (because not all 'practising Christians' really trust Jesus) it still means that you might look at a group queuing up at the supermarket checkouts and be reasonably hopeful of it containing a Christian or two. Reassuring, isn't it?

But get this: according to the same survey, half the population do not know a practising Christian. And even those who do know a Christian don't know them well enough to have a spiritual conversation. Practising

1. https://www.ons.gov.uk/peoplepopulationandcommunity/ culturalidentity/religion/bulletins/religionenglandandwales/census2021. Accessed 12 December 2023.

2. https://talkingjesus.org/2022-research/ *Accessed 20 March 2023.*

5

Christians are practically invisible to 50 per cent of people in the UK.

On an average Sunday, 98 per cent of the UK population is not inside an evangelical church. Whether you go with any of the ideas in this book or not, this is the stark reality we have to face. This means that in my town of about 40,000 people, no more than 800 will be in a church where they will hear the gospel; 39,200 of the townspeople will not. Do the numbers for where you live, or even just for your street. Doesn't it move something in you to wonder if we could do more to reach them?

We may start with our family and our friends, the people we work with, and those we 'do life' with. We may witness through the outreach of our local church and we may teach all ages about Jesus. But we often do not move beyond that.

But if we are to fulfil Jesus' command to 'Go' there must be some further outward movement. It must include a displacement from here to there. Of course, there is an 'all nations' element to this trajectory; we need to be world Christians, seeing every people, tribe, and tongue as our mission field, and employing the expertise and contacts of mission agencies to facilitate the local church's sending of its members to reach the lost across the globe. But nearer to home, it means crossing other boundaries to make the gospel known – moving outside the church to eventually bring them inside.

We must progress from our local contacts to our workplaces and schools, but further still to our high streets and beaches. We must go from door to door and to our centres of philosophy and learning; to the online and offline communities, from tablet to smartphone, and to anywhere that people gather. We must go local and national.

I wrote this book for people who want to think about how we become more *visible*; how we get the gospel to the vast majority around us who don't know a Christian yet. It's for those who want to think through some ideas on how we get into the *marketplace* – the everyday lives, ideas, imaginations and ideologies of people who will never bump into us on the street.

Please understand: I in no way wish to diminish the importance of personal evangelism or church gatherings where we preach the gospel. But just as the apostles and early church began in the synagogues, among those who already had a very real spiritual interest, but then ventured far beyond such places and people, I am calling on us too, to go much further than those places where people gather who already have some interest in what we have to say.

Yes, we know that God is sovereign and He has given us the contacts we already have, and we need to start there. We know it's not about techniques and methods or a slick marketing campaign, and the gospel will only bear fruit if the Holy Spirit is at work.

But the danger in knowing it is not in our power to make people believe is that we may end up making no effort and having no plan. We may content ourselves with putting on a few events and asking some of our friends and family along now and then.

What I hope is that this book will spur us on to make an effort and develop a plan.

This is not a book for 'professionals' who can gain a profile in the national media while the rest of us pray from the sidelines and send financial donations. It's less of a 'how-to-do-it' book and more about the principle and possibilities, together with some examples, so that you might then seek to apply these in your own context with the gifts and opportunities you have.

This, then, is a book for ordinary Christians to think through how to reach more people with the good news. What can I do and how do I support those who are pioneering connections to make Christ more visible?

The roadmap

To help you navigate this book, here's a description of the journey.

We will start in chapter one with a definition of the marketplace and how we can witness there in a variety of ways.

In the marketplace we will meet all kinds of ideas, questions, and objections. So in chapter two we will consider what some of these ideas are and what kind of conversations could result, and how we might navigate them. Because the gospel is true it can be defended from a logical and evidential point of view. It's not just about feeling the conviction of our calling; we also need a degree of confidence that the gospel is relevant and powerful – it really does work – and that it has power to save and transform lives (Rom. 1:16).

Then in the final four chapters we will consider methods of taking the message out, some very ancient and others very contemporary, from street preaching to broadcast and social media. I want to encourage many more people to get involved. For some of you, this will be new and exciting and maybe on a bigger scale than you have ever experienced (these days it isn't as hard to break into as you might think).

Others of you reading this book may be inspired to grow a network of contacts for you and your church, confident that you can have these kinds of conversations. You don't need any special training; you just need the

Word of God, His Holy Spirit, and your own willingness to serve.

I have no great theological qualifications, so as I wrote I was thinking about all the different kinds of people I have met on my journey so far. And I was writing for people like me – and you – who live and work and socialise with people who are not Christians yet.

Finally, I confess that I am not doing all the things I talk about in this book. I am not even doing some of the things I could easily do. I am at times fearful, lazy, and lacking in compassion. But I have done most of the things I have written about at least once, and some I have done a lot!

All of us can be a part of reaching the millions who are lost in the UK. We just need to find our place. My prayer is that you will be inspired and feel accountable as we go through this journey together.

Questions for reflection and discussion

1. What does the Great Commission (Matt. 28:16-20) mean to you?

2. How do you feel about the people in your town who may not know any Christians? Is your attitude an appropriate one for a Christian to have?

3. Do you have any ideas about how you might be able to reach people you currently do not know?

Chapter 1
The Marketplace

'While Paul was waiting for them in Athens, he was greatly distressed to see that the city was full of idols. So he reasoned in the synagogue with both Jews and God-fearing Greeks, as well as in the marketplace day by day with those who happened to be there. A group of Epicurean and Stoic philosophers began to debate with him. Some of them asked, "What is this babbler trying to say?" Others remarked, "He seems to be advocating foreign gods." They said this because Paul was preaching the good news about Jesus and the resurrection.'
(Acts 17:16-18)

A market town

When I was a child, my dad was a farmer, and pretty much every Tuesday he would take a few newborn calves for sale to the market in Haywards Heath in the south-east of England.[1] During the school holidays I loved going with him. Everything was fascinating: the sights, sounds, and smells of so many animals in one place, from enormous

---

1. Interestingly, the market was founded around 1859 and became one of the largest in the south of England, running for 120 years before closing in 1989. The founder became a local entrepreneur and philanthropist. He was a land and property valuer, local councillor, Justice of the Peace and President of the cricket club – a great example of someone who was part of his community, which is what this book is all about!

bulls to rabbits and guinea pigs; the excitement of the auction with the mysterious language and semaphore of the bidding; the many market stalls surrounding the main arena with all kinds of junk for sale.

I happen to live in that same town now but the market and its magic have long gone. There is now a Sainsbury's supermarket where it once stood – a temple to consumerism and a market for mostly processed food. It is a meeting place of sorts but is not at the heart of the community in the same way.

But there are still places where local people gather. The marketplace is now broken up between a variety of physical and virtual spaces. These gathering places may be real street corners and public halls or, increasingly, many different venues in the online world.

I want to suggest in this chapter that, alongside all our other vital church outreach programmes, we need to make sure to spend some time 'reasoning in our marketplaces' as the Apostle Paul did. Let's consider how he did it.

Paul in Athens

In Acts 17 Luke tells us about Paul's second missionary journey, through the cities of Thessalonica, Berea, and on to Athens. It is not clear whether he had actually planned to go to Athens because he was basically chased out of Thessalonica by the Jews and some local mercenaries they had hired. Whatever Paul may have purposed to do, this was no diversion as God used his rejection in these other cities to move him on to Athens, where Paul made excellent use of his time for the good of its residents – and also for our benefit as we read about it today.

Paul's speech in Athens is one of the best known in Acts as an example of the contextualisation of the gospel message for a pagan audience.[2] There are many great lessons to draw from his method of both winsomely connecting with their culture but, at the same time, not mincing his words as he concludes by declaring that God 'commands all people everywhere to repent' (17:30). Is that how you are supposed to end a seeker-friendly evangelistic message? Paul evidently thinks so!

How did he find himself engaging with such influential people on such a stage? It all started in the marketplace of the city. He was motivated to talk to anyone, and this was where they gathered. That sparked off a debate with some philosophers which then led to the invitation to address the *Areopagus*, the council of leaders and thinkers who ruled the city.

Athens was one of the great cities of the ancient world. Its impact and significance had somewhat dwindled under the Roman empire, yet it remained a centre of learning and its history made it a place of great renown. It was the city that gave us the concept and language of democracy, philosophy, theatre, and architecture. This was the cultural capital of the world – the ancient equivalent of London, New York, Tokyo, or Paris.[3] The philosophers Socrates, Plato, Aristotle, and Epicurus spent time there and changed the way much of the world thought and reasoned.

These days the whole area is a massive archaeological site. Men and women with trowels dig through ruins while labourers demolish modern streets and houses to expose even more buildings and artefacts underneath, seeking to reconstruct what it would have looked like in ancient times.

---

2.   So suggests Martin Salter in his forthcoming commentary on Acts: *The Hodder Bible Commentary: Acts* (London: Hodder, 2024).

3.   John, Stott, *The Message of Acts* (IVP, UK 1991), p. 276

We already know much of that picture. As Paul looked about him it would have provoked a sense of awe. There was the Acropolis, the fortified city on the hill, at the centre of which was the Parthenon, a magnificent temple dedicated to the goddess Athena, with a great statue of her, holding a gleaming spear twelve metres high, which could be seen forty miles away. Elsewhere across the city there were representations of Apollo, Jupiter, Venus, Mercury, Bacchus and Neptune. Then there was the Areopagus – a hill dedicated to Ares, the Greek god of war. (The Romans called him Mars so the location is often referred to as 'Mars Hill'.)

But Paul wasn't an awestruck tourist, trying to get the perfect montage of pictures to post on Instagram. As he observed and reflected on what he saw, he was 'distressed to see so many idols' (17:16). The Greek word used to describe his response was sometimes used as a medical term for struggling to breathe. We might say he was choked up – apoplectic, or 'spitting feathers'.

This extreme distress was because he saw past the impressive appearance of the effigies of the gods to what they signified: idolatry. The statues were physical representations of fictional deities, whom the ordinary people attempted to placate and serve. The city was full of them; it was reportedly 'easier to find a god there than a man'.[4]

Why wouldn't he be distressed? The true God was ignored while vast wealth and effort was devoted to make-believe gods. And all the while the masses were oblivious to the truth and rooting their hopes in a fantasy.

Therefore, driven by his deeply felt concern, Paul spoke to the people of Athens in the places where they met. Day after day he entered the synagogue, speaking to Jews and God-fearing Greeks, and visited the town square

---

4. Copan, Paul and Litwak, Kenneth D., *The Gospel in the Marketplace of Ideas* (InterVarsity Press, 2014), p. 30

(the marketplace) to speak with anyone who was willing to listen.

The marketplace

The agora was the name for the marketplace in Athens. Markets, then and now, are where people gather and an interchange of various kinds takes place: goods and services for money, alongside opinions, news, and gossip. In Paul's day (especially in Greek cities), they were at the centre of social, commercial and civic life and acted as meeting places for public speeches, political hustings, sporting events, religious services, and theatrical performances. It was the people's town hall, main street, leisure centre, cinema complex, Amazon, Google, BBC News, and GOD TV, all in one location!

The agora hosted formal ceremonies, government business, and was also where farmers and craftsmen could sell cattle, grain, meat, fish, fruit, vegetables, cheese, eggs, honey, and wine. Artisans would trade pottery, household goods, clothing, and textiles (often with bright colours and decorative designs). More expensive items could be purchased such as gems, silks, and wool. It was also a place for the trading of human slaves.

All life was here. Citizens mingled with foreigners (including a significant Jewish population); rich and poor, the social elite and slaves; moneychangers, bankers, judges and criminals, philosophers and merchants. People new in town would come here to find people to trade with or to form alliances. Practically everyone visited the agora.

Paul had recent bad experience of other Greek marketplaces: they were places for the execution of rough justice (Acts 16:19) and where a mob could be gathered to stir up trouble (Acts 17:5).

Philosophers in the marketplace

The agora was also a place for trading big ideas about the world, and Athens, in particular, was the heart and soul of Greek philosophy with many competing worldviews. In the fourth century B.C. Plato had set up a school of philosophy in the city. One of his students, Aristotle, later went on to educate Alexander the Great. Other schools of thought included the Epicureans and the Stoics, both of whom engaged with Paul in his marketplace discussions, leading to his being brought to the Areopagus, the scene of his famous speech in Acts 17:22-31.

These philosophers had some sense of a transcendent being or thought at the heart of the universe, but adapted their thought under the influence of the Roman empire's pantheon of many gods. They believed in the human soul but were less clear about it continuing into the afterlife; neither group believed in a bodily resurrection or final judgment.

Epicurus (c. 341-270 B.C.) founded a school of philosophy that stressed the pursuit of pleasure in a world of pain and uncertainty as the ultimate good. As we are all going to die, we should make the most of the short time that we have; self-control and the acquiring of knowledge would help to give meaning to life. He stressed the importance of friendships – joining with others of like mind for emotional support and companionship – to achieve happiness. Human beings are the product of a chance combination of atoms and so, as death is just the end of all existence, it is not to be feared. 'Death is nothing to us', Epicurus said.

Professor Bryan Magee writes that 'What is striking about Epicureanism is how similar it is, point by point, to the scientific and liberal humanism of the twentieth century'.[5] It does all sound remarkably contemporary, doesn't it?

Stoicism was an ancient Greek school of philosophy founded at Athens by Zeno (334-262 B.C.) of Cyprus. It taught the development of self-control and fortitude as a means of overcoming destructive emotions and that becoming a clear and unbiased thinker allowed one to understand the universal reason (what they often called the 'logos'). It called for a determination to face the trials and tragedies of life with an 'unruffled acceptance',[6] in the belief that we cannot change whatever will be. Stoics saw the body as a prison from which we escape at death; the divine spark returns to the cosmic logos and we become one with nature.

Stoicism as we know it today has become, for many people, '...a secular substitute for religious belief, [seeking] to both fill the meaning gap left in the absence of belief in God and to serve as a coping mechanism for negative experiences, failures, and even the knowledge of one's eventual death. In the absence of the resurrection, Stoicism becomes a palatable option for those seeking to navigate the highs and lows of an uncertain and increasingly hostile world.'[7] One such popular proponent of this teaching today is Jordan Peterson.

When Paul addresses these philosophers at the Areopagus, he begins with a direct contradiction of the Epicurean theory about how the world began: 'The God who made the world and everything in it...' (Acts 17:24). He then seems to reference the Stoic poet Seneca, as at times he agrees with but also critiques their philosophy. He also quotes directly from a Greek poet called Aratus, which would have worked well for his audience.

5.   Magee, Bryan, *The Story of Philosophy* (Dorling Kindersley, 1998), p. 45

6.   Magee, *The Story of Philosophy*, p. 46

7.   https://www.thegospelcoalition.org/article/christianity-challenges-stoic-spirit/ Accessed 12 December 2023.

The audience

The people Paul spoke to in the marketplace were not all philosophers. He spoke to 'those who happened to be there': a market trader, a careful shopper, a farmer, a street entertainer – the deep thinkers and the big buyers. Just like today, the big thinkers in science and philosophy had some influence on popular belief, as their ideas trickled down to the masses, but, for most people who were just getting on with their lives, the real shapers of their worldview were the inherited tales and myths, and the traditional wisdom and assumptions of family and culture.

So the everyday people in Athens worshipped many gods. These Greek or Roman deities were not dreamt up in philosophical textbooks but found in the stories, poems and plays that captured the popular imagination. Famous playwrights in Athens such as Sophocles – the screenwriters, actors, and producers of their day – both reflected popular beliefs and shaped them, much as they do today. The city was named after Athena, the goddess of wisdom, daughter of Zeus. She won the honour after competing with another god, Poseidon (he was a sea god and his consolation prize was to have a very average film about a shipwreck named after him).

The locals would be entertained by the epic tales of the fighting and sordid interactions between these gods, behaviour which would make *Game of Thrones* seem rather tame; all this alongside the hero cults, mystery religions with secret rituals, veneration of their ancestors as demi-gods, and the worship of the *Agnostos Theos* – the unknown god—just in case they had missed one of the gods and he or she might be upset.

All this popular entertainment and spirituality would have influenced the thinking and the cultural values of the people Paul talked with in the marketplace. It is no different today; the stories we tell each other and the things that entertain us can significantly shape us even unknowingly.

Reasoning

Witnessing all of this – the life, culture, and spirituality of Athens – Paul did more than feel great distress. He could have merely fumed inside. In our day he might have expressed his outrage by posting about it to let off steam.

No, he didn't just lament; he *engaged* with people as he talked to them in their places of worship and in their streets and squares. Acts 17 reads that 'he reasoned in the synagogue with both Jews and God-fearing Greeks, as well as in the marketplace day by day with those who happened to be there' (v. 17).

Notice that he did not give up at the first hurdle. He went back there every day, bringing more evidence, answering more questions. In the synagogue and in the marketplace, Paul wanted to make the most of every opportunity, and to create openings for the gospel where they didn't seem to exist.

He went to the religious (Jews and God-fearing Greeks), to the intellectuals and to the everyday market people, and he reasoned with them – every day.

Our marketplace

Just as in Paul's day, the people around us worship many gods. They worship deities conjured up in the entertainment they consume – the stories our culture tells in its novels, films, and on celebrity social media platforms. Some high-profile personalities acknowledge a 'higher power', but often it exists only to support their own self-promotion and speed them on their journey to personal fulfilment, comfort, and success.

Some worship at the altar of career, family, or the pursuit of pleasure; nothing deflects them from these all-consuming commitments and their packed diaries tell the tale of daily service to their god.

So where are the marketplaces at which people gather in our day? The intersection of people's lives is now more complex and less restricted to physical settings. It may still be an actual place, but not necessarily.

Wherever political discourse, commerce, entertainment, or socialising takes place, there is our equivalent marketplace. It could be an actual market square – there are a few still around in our towns and cities and on good weather days people might stop and chat informally. They may also be the place where organised rallies, protests, or other forms of mass gathering take place.

Plenty of other situations provide opportunity for ad hoc conversations and interaction: the local supermarket aisle, the queue at the post office, the kebab stall, the coffee shop, the arrival at the front door of the post woman or Amazon delivery man – even the stands of the local football club on a Saturday afternoon, or the music festival weekend. And then there are the streets by our modern temples to materialism and entertainment. There are even traders there, along with campaigners and entertainers. It is everywhere.

But there are other marketplaces where people gather. We meet not just on the street, but in the cloud! Offline and online. Old media, new media, local media, and national media, and the large monster that is social media, along with all the person-to-person interactions is our agora. We conduct business in person and at the push of a button. We do local politics on the streets and in town halls but also in online forums, X (formerly Twitter) campaigns, and with our followers on social media.

In Paul's day, Athens was a multicultural city; today we live in a multicultural society and an online community that touches every corner of the globe. Then, Athens was a melting pot of philosophical, religious, and spiritual ideas; now it is just the same. Then, ordinary people didn't think very deeply about philosophy, but they drank deeply the ideologies of their day and lived them out, often without even being aware of it; we live in an age when our values and ideals are shaped by the media and by entertainment more than by literature, education, or authority figures but, as in first-century Athens, the influence is often unconscious and powerful.

This is our world, and these are its marketplaces – different, yet not so different from the ones Paul visited.

Take your distress into the marketplace

Wherever communities gather today is a marketplace and we need to be there too. The reality is, however, that we are not very present. Religious voices are there, as are the promoters of all manner of philosophies. But mostly the witnesses to the gospel of Jesus keep their heads down. What holds us back from visiting?

The marketplace I went to as a child was a scary place: big, noisy animals, men with big coats and big hands, and dodgy-looking market traders. I tried to look confident, but I didn't really know what to do and where to go. I didn't know the cultural expectations. I was in a town in which I could easily have got lost, a place where hardly anybody knew me. I feared I might bid for something with an accidental gesture and have to come home with a cow. But it was OK – my dad was with me. He knew what to do. He held me with his chubby, work-hardened hands and kept me safe.

Like me as a child, are we a bit scared to enter today's marketplaces?

Sometimes stepping out feels high risk – we're not quite sure how to behave and what is expected of us. We're not sure how to interact; we fear being exposed and rejected.

Our marketplace might be a daunting place to visit, but we go there because Jesus commands us to do so. It might be a bewildering place at first, but Jesus is with us. It might seem intimidating, but we go because we are compelled by the love of Christ.

Are you distressed by the idols you observe in the culture all around you? Are you moved by the sin and the ignorance? It is there in the idolatry implicit, and often explicit, in the awesome technology, great artistic artefacts and spectacular entertainment performances, which call for people's worship and allegiance. It is there, too, in more subtle ways in the form of the beliefs, values, hopes, and dreams of ordinary men and women going about their daily lives. In western cultures especially, this idolatry manifests itself in materialism, the pursuit of success and relationships, and self-identity. In other cultures, those idols might be a desire for honour, status, or the quest for transcendent peace.[8]

So, yes, what we see does distress us, and we can diagnose the problem well.

But the question is, as you observe all this, will your depth of concern and sorrow drive you out of the bunker and into the open? Are you willing to engage in the public square, to speak up in meetings and on the Internet? Will you speak to your family, friends and neighbours and then move out onto social media and even traditional broadcast forums? Will you challenge the accepted

8. See: Salter, *Acts*, forthcoming.

cultural narratives with a better story of love and hope and a God of justice and mercy?

It won't be easy; it may start badly. You may be misunderstood. In Acts 17 we read that some people mistook Paul's use of the word 'resurrection' for the name of a 'foreign god' and others described him as a 'babbler' – the Greek word means a 'seed-picker' – a bird feeding on scraps. He was not getting his message across!

My first ever interview on national radio was for BBC Radio 4. The person I debated was Alice Roberts, a patron for 'Humanists UK'. I did a reasonable but not exceptional job of arguing that an innate moral understanding in society points to the reality of an author of that morality above and beyond human existence. Professor Roberts argued that 'humanists look to scientific evidence and reason to understand the world. And they place human welfare and happiness – as well as the welfare of other sentient animals – at the heart of how they choose to live their life.' My point was that there is no reason to think of welfare as a societal good unless there is a God who has set such a standard for us. Alice Roberts and many others like her enjoy the fruit without acknowledging the root – an inherited morality which they use as a standard by which to assess good and evil. Maybe she had Christian parents that helped form her outlook, and maybe Christian grandparents too, not to mention a whole history and heritage of Christian culture in the UK.[9]

In the immediate aftermath of the radio debate, her followers on X ridiculed me because she, a famous TV academic, had 395,000 followers and I had just a few hundred and, in any case, I was talking rubbish compared to this famous intellectual. I was the seed-picker, the gutter sparrow.

---

9. https://www.spectator.co.uk/article/alice-roberts-and-the-problem-with-humanism/ *Accessed 3 May 2023.*

That sort of first experience of engaging in the marketplace can be intimidating! In Athens, Paul's initial poor showing did not stop him; and his persistence in the marketplace, day after day, bore fruit in important conversations which ultimately led to his 'promotion' from the marketplace to the big stage, an invitation to address the philosophers at Mars Hill.

This persistence paid off. Not all of Athens was converted but some believed (Acts 17:34). What for Paul started in the marketplace with misunderstanding and mockery ended with rejoicing in heaven over sinners repenting.

What about us? Will we, like Paul in Athens, keep going, day after day, even if at first it doesn't go well? We all fear rejection because we have a need to be valued, but if we find our worth and sense of identity in our status in Christ, we will be enabled to carry on, secure in Him.

We may feel inadequate to share the gospel; will we know what to say or how to answer questions that may come up? But we can train ourselves in these matters and we must also depend on the Holy Spirit to help us speak wisely.

In our streets and in today's marketplace of ideas and idolatries, the gospel *will* get through to some. We can know the joy of one day meeting new believers who are such because we kept going, day after day, speaking to whoever will listen.

This is what is so exciting about the marketplace.

Questions for reflection and discussion

1. Where might be your marketplaces? Do you go there?

2. What holds you back from engaging in gospel conversations in your marketplaces?

3. Do you believe it is worth the effort of stepping out into the marketplace? Is it likely to bear fruit? Why, or why not?

Chapter 2

Market Dialogue

'Let your conversation be always full of grace,
seasoned with salt,
so that you may know how to answer everyone.'
(Colossians 4:6)

How do you start a conversation? These days, what even qualifies as a conversation? A WhatsApp chat? A Facebook Messenger exchange? A comment on a post?

Just as there are multiple manifestations of the marketplace, as we saw in chapter one, so there are multiple channels by which to engage in those spaces. They all count as communication and they each have their benefits and some limitations.

This chapter focuses less on the channels but on the *content*. With the conviction that we need to be having conversations, what then are we likely to be talking about in our discussions, presentations, debates, and messages back and forth? How will we show people that if they take the time to consider the gospel they will find that it makes sense? What could we say? How would we respond to their antagonism and scepticism?

We have already seen that in Athens Paul's instinct was to faithfully 'reason' with people in his marketplace – the ancient equivalent of our modern places of trade, entertainment, socialising, politics, and religion. Let's delve a bit deeper into what it means to 'reason'.

We need to talk

The word used for 'reasoned' in Acts 17 is the Greek word *dialego* which obviously sounds a lot like our word 'dialogue'. Its meaning is not exactly the same, but *dialego* certainly includes the idea of a conversation – interactive discussion. It can also mean to dispute – as the disciples did when they reasoned about which among them was the greatest (e.g. Luke 9:46) – but also to logically lay out an argument, to give a speech that carefully seeks to get a point across.

For Paul, and also for us, the purpose is to get God's point across – to lead people to the truth about Christ. For example, the word is often used to describe Paul's speaking in a synagogue or lecture hall, showing to the Jews and God-fearers how the Old Testament finds its fulfilment in Christ. It describes a style of address that is similar to, but not quite the same as, preaching.

As we know, Paul often preached – proclaiming and declaring the good news of Jesus. But that's not what he is doing here; he is *reasoning*, this being the other main method of engaging with people that he used regularly (e.g. Acts 17:2). I expect that's how it went at the synagogue in Athens – more like what we would call a seminar followed up by a Q&A.

Then in the market we can imagine his reasoning was more of a free-flowing dialogue with purpose. There amongst the traders calling attention to their bargains, people catching up with gossip and the street entertainers, came Paul. Speaking with ones and twos, or with a small gathering around him, he got into a discussion – a dialogue – presenting his case. He argued for the logic, the evidence, and the unrivalled beauty of the good news about Jesus the true God, risen from the dead. Maybe at times it was more of a monologue, as people stood and listened to Paul, and at other times more of a full-on debate with arguments back and forth.

We don't know how these conversations began; maybe some started as people asked him questions because he was an outsider; maybe he set up a lectern, started speaking, and hoped for a crowd to gather. Or maybe he just went up to groups of shoppers and said, 'Hey, how's it going? It's another scorcher, isn't it? What's the local news? Do you have a faith? What do you think makes for a great leader? What are your hopes and fears? What makes for a good life? How are your gods working out for you?'

What we do know is that Paul was noticed; he got people's attention. The crowds discussed his ideas and he provoked a debate among the Epicureans and Stoics who asked themselves, 'What is this man talking about?'

Notice that whatever method of introduction and style of debate Paul used, he always used *words*. Authentic, obedient Christian living and the love of God expressed in our actions can be a powerful demonstration of the truth of the gospel. Conversely, an inconsistent life will damage our testimony.

Those closest to us will watch how we live and then decide whether they want to listen to the words we speak. We should always seek to honour our Lord and Saviour with our lives, and there should be many contexts, in relationship with others, where this is part of our witness.

But it is never enough only to testify with a godly life. You cannot reason or have a dialogue without words. And sometimes we just don't have the opportunity or time to develop an ongoing relationship with someone so that they feel the impact of our lives.

We have to do more than just live – we need to *confess*. We need to have a dialogue, and sometimes to proclaim truth. In the public square we have to accept that – certainly in one-off or initial encounters – the life lived is less prominent, and our words and body language are the main ways in which people encounter us. People in the marketplace (including the 50 per cent of the UK population who don't know a Christian), will not have a chance to observe how we live day-to-day. In a random encounter with you, a person will hear your words and maybe get a brief first impression of your character. They may never see you again but in that moment they will have received a slice of the gospel message and will need to decide whether to consider the matter any further and look any deeper. So, we are not to be mime artists – we need to have a *conversation*.

Conversation starters

But how do we get those conversations started?

I left school when I was sixteen and did an engineering apprenticeship. In my first year I trained with young men, mostly my own age, who smoked weed in their break times, got drunk at the weekend, and talked a lot about their exploits with the opposite sex. Later I worked on a factory floor with people who were older, many with families, but whose language was even more crude than the apprentices. Eventually I got some more qualifications and ended up working with university graduates and more conceptual thinkers. Later still I rubbed shoulders with business owners who were millionaires. I cannot claim I was a great witness and I can't boast a long list of converts, but I can honestly say I tried with a lot of them to speak about Jesus.

My simple observation from all of these encounters is that most people are willing to talk and the best way to have a good gospel conversation is to start one. Yes, different interests and educational backgrounds have to be taken into consideration, but everyone has the same spiritual need and those without Christ usually tend to make pretty much the same objections. I have found this to be true whether I am in one-to one conversations on the street or dialoguing in the broadcast media.

The way into such exchanges will vary depending on the person being addressed. Even with those we know well we still need to start somewhere. In talking with a good friend we may find that a spiritual subject arises easily as we talk about life. With a work colleague whom we know only a little, it will require more effort to steer the conversation. If we are chatting with a person in the street whom we hardly know at all but sometimes pass the time of day with, it may feel like a major effort to drop the 'God bomb' into the mix.

Many different opportunities can arise in the course of our lives. It might be that guy you got to know while gaming online, with whom you have only ever discussed tactics and pizza. It could be someone responding to your social media post, blog, or something you submitted to a local news website. It could be a small group listening as we make a presentation on the street. It could be someone reading our posts or blogs, or something we submitted to a local news website; or someone who listens to us on a phone-in as we give a Christian perspective; or someone engaging with us on the many and various individual and group messaging systems.

God is not calling us to become great orators or debaters. But we are all capable of having a conversation even with people we don't know – maybe gently disagreeing with another's point or correcting their misunderstanding of something we have said. Some of those conversations will be with our friends and families. But why not also venture out and have those conversations out there, in the marketplace?

This may well mean that we initiate the conversation by doing the talking and leading the dialogue. This will probably lead on to us being questioned and challenged about what we believe and we need to be open to this and willing to engage. Sometimes we will be the ones asking the questions. I wonder if Paul asked any during his debates?

Asking questions is a good way into a dialogue. Randy Newman, in his book *Questioning Evangelism*[1], suggests that the best way to share the gospel is not by directly telling people what to believe, but by asking questions which then engages them in meaningful conversations. It has the advantage of not just helping us understand where people are at, but also shows we are interested in them as people.

This is not a new idea; Jesus Himself provided a masterclass on this approach when He got into conversation with the Samaritan woman at the well (John 4:4-30). Jesus had a clear purpose in view. He used questions to draw from the woman her deepfelt desire for something satisfying, something lasting, and ultimately showed her that what she sought could be found only in Him. He had never met her before and He wasn't doing relational evangelism, doing life with her for a few years, and popping in a few choice morsels along the way in the hope of getting a bite. He might never meet her again; time was short. He didn't rush but He made the most of His short time with her. He was reasoning in the marketplace. And so can we.

---

1. Newman, Randy, *Questioning Evangelism* (Kregel, 2023) 3rd ed.

However, we should be aware that sometimes direct questions are not the best approach, because the person being addressed may find them intimidating. So we need to be alert to potential insensitivity in the way we engage. And we also need to recognise that sometimes asking questions isn't appropriate because it's just not that kind of conversation.

Finally, asking questions is a method we can use in many different settings, even when it is just us speaking. Posing questions that the reader/hearer might be asking (or ought to be asking) in a piece of writing, or a sermon, or even in an interview for the media, is a way of creating a dialogue even without anyone else being directly involved.

From sympathy to hostility

So, we get into a conversation about something to do with our faith. How will we be received, and what might we end up talking about?

On his various missionary journeys, Paul did not get a very sympathetic hearing. For us, amongst our friends and family, we may still receive some degree of an open door to speak if there exists among them a legacy of respect for our faith. But in the UK and the west more generally, at the public and political level, sympathy for orthodox Christianity has declined very significantly.

In an article for the 'First Things'[2] website in February 2022, Aaron Renn wrote about the shift over the last fifty years or so in public attitudes to Christianity in the USA, from *sympathy* (before 1994) to *apathy* (1994–2014) and since then to *hostility*.

---

2.   https://www.firstthings.com/article/2022/02/the-three-worlds-of-evangelicalism *Accessed 3 May 2023.*

Renn suggested that, for most of the last century up to the 1990s, to be known as a Christian was an indicator of upstanding citizenship; faith in the God of the Bible was a status-enhancer and Christian moral norms were pretty much in line with a wider understanding of morality. People believed these standards were right even if they didn't necessarily follow them themselves. People in public life who transgressed might therefore experience negative consequences.

For the next decade or so, a shift took place whereby society took more of a neutral stance towards Christianity – the *apathy* stage. Faith no longer had a privileged status but to be known as a Christian had limited impact on one's social standing either way; Christians were mostly just ignored. While Christian moral norms retained some residual influence in society – for example, Christian marriage was still popular and seen as an ideal by an older generation – the moral framework was shifting rapidly. My experience, growing up in the 1960s and '70s, was that the transition away from Christianity being considered a benign influence was already well under way.

We are all aware that in more recent years society has come to have a negative and even hostile view of our evangelical faith, especially its objective moral standard and exclusive claims for salvation. In society's elite circles, Christian morality is regularly denounced as a threat to the public good and human flourishing. To advocate such views is therefore likely to invite very negative consequences. The modern-day Epicureans and Stoics will call us the equivalent of 'seed-pickers' and much worse. The attacks will come from both religious and secular groups; leaders of both will decry our 'fundamentalist', 'bigoted', and 'extremist' views. But even away from the influencers, amongst 'ordinary people' the news and entertainment media they consume promotes 'progressive' ideas such as individual freedom and fulfilment is the way to find meaning in life, having sex is a basic human need and right, family loyalty is good until it isn't working for me, and death is to be avoided and ignored.

Although Renn is writing from a North American perspective, his three categories definitely parallel the UK experience, but sadly we seem to be twenty or thirty years ahead of his timeline. Facing all this hostility is already a reality for anyone willing to speak up.

So it will be tough. We need to be ready for that. Because of our Christian beliefs we may experience intimidation, psychological pressure, marginalisation, and 'cancelling' – exclusion from some parts of public life.

But we also need to have some perspective. People have occasionally said to me that the Great Commission is really hard for us to fulfil today because of our hostile environment. But I have to remind them and myself that the apostles and the early church faced opposition on a scale unknown even to us in the West right now. Indeed, compared to the physical violence, imprisonment, and martyrdom suffered by the worldwide church throughout history and very much today, the opposition we face is relatively insignificant.

Worldviews

I walk my dog every morning. I know quite a few people on my route, but in most cases I don't know their (or their dogs') names. I pass the time of day with them, talking about the weather or our dogs or even something in the news. But were I to ask my dog-walking friends to explain their worldview they would likely start taking a different route for their morning exercise. It's mostly only philosophers and Christians who think in terms of worldviews. But everyone has one; you only have to start a conversation with someone on pretty much any topic and it will soon become clear that this is so.

Everyone has things they value. Everyone has their sources of authority. Everyone has some views on the fundamental questions of our existence: what is right and wrong? What is life all about? What happens when we die? They might not have a conscious system of belief, but it is there under the surface and every day they make decisions based on it.

People might not use technical terms like 'deist' or 'humanist' but they will express such views in other words. So someone will say, 'I believe in God and I think He is like …'. Another will suggest the vague view that there is 'something out there' controlling their destiny. Alternatively, others will say that science and reason provide the only guide to understanding reality and that all supernatural explanations are off limits; human beings are just complex machines and physical matter is all that exists. As far as what this means for how we should then live, the conclusion is often that nothing really matters, there is no absolute truth, and so the only way to live is to enjoy ourselves in the moment.

But have those who think like this really thought through all the philosophical ramifications of their godless, meaningless, hopeless world? Nearly everyone believes in right and wrong, but most don't really know why. They approve of showing empathy and kindness to others, and that we should seek the good of all humanity and that family is important. Yet why should any of these things be so? They feel them to be obvious at some level and yet this certainty seems at odds with a universe that is closed, with no external standard of morality outside of ourselves.

In other words, whether we talk in terms of worldviews or not, they do exist and in talking to people we need to try to understand their underlying thinking in order to know how to address them – to question and critique their thinking in terms and categories that they will recognise and understand. Only then will we be able to challenge them in ways that will hit home.

So first we need to be willing to do some work, to think about what people value and how they make decisions.

Battle lines

Let's be optimistic and assume for a moment that you have got into a meaningful conversation with someone. It might be private, or public. It could be face to face or through a keyboard. You might be asking the questions and seeking to understand the other's worldview or you may be the one being interviewed or cross-examined. Whichever situation you face, it is likely that there will be a set of specific issues which, in our current social and moral environment, will come up. In my experience and in talking with people who do evangelism as their day job, the same questions come up over and over again. What follows are those top seven anti-Christian missiles with my own suggestions for how to respond to them.

Although you can read plenty of books and websites on apologetics, which will go into much more detail than I do here, these are a few of the main arguments for easy reference. Some of them may seem rather obscure or technical, but I can say that dropping them into conversations (especially in media interviews) can be highly effective at disrupting the attack and causing those listening in to realise that there are other ways of looking at the issue in question.

Identity, sexuality, and gender

Is God Anti-Gay?[3] is a helpful book by Sam Allberry with a great title because it is indeed the question we might often be asked: 'Does God care about gay people or does He just hate them?' It's a personalising question; the issue is not whether God has a view on homosexuality in the abstract, but whether He has a specific, strong reaction against such people. It's an emotional question; not whether something is right and wrong but how people, and God Himself, 'feel'. It's also a questioning of identity because 'gay' is used by those who ask us this question as descriptive of an identity, an immutable characteristic – like asking whether God hates short people or black people.

Some friends of ours were recently on holiday and made friends with some other couples. One evening in the flow of a conversation they were asked whether they thought homosexuality was wrong, a sin. When they responded that it was, the questioner immediately got up and left. This is not a rare occurrence. This is an emotive topic and can feel like the one area we don't want to be asked about.

When I was a teenager in the 1970s and '80s this would definitely not have been an issue to challenge Christians about. Back then 'gay' was used as an insult. By the 1990s homosexuality was becoming more widely debated with questions such as whether people were born gay, but it was probably still viewed negatively by the majority. More celebrities were 'coming out' (or being 'outed') but that wave of sympathy and support that is a feature of such happenings now was not apparent then. In contrast, today, the prevailing attitude is very much that being gay is as natural and normal as being heterosexual, and if you are attracted to someone of the same sex you should feel

---

3. Allberry, Sam, *Is God Anti-Gay?* (Good Book Company, 2023) 2nd edition.

free and safe to own that as your core identity and live out a gay lifestyle, if you so desire.

The current consensus is less clear when it comes to transgender rights, especially about whether children should be allowed to transition and whether 'safe spaces' should be provided for women into which males presenting as females should not be allowed. But even here, the debate tends to focus more on these secondary issues about potential harms, rather than whether transitioning is morally acceptable at all.

So as you can see, the cards are definitely stacked against us on the subject of identity, sexuality, and gender.

Homosexuality is the most common topic that comes up when I have been interviewed in the media; even if the discussion begins on some other topic it often gets hijacked by a hostile interviewer or other participant raising what they consider to be the 'gotcha' question, to which there is apparently only one acceptable answer. Answering these kinds of questions is extremely tricky. We might be tempted to avoid the question by suggesting that there is a different and more important issue to discuss. But sometimes we just have to stand up for what we believe.

So where do we begin? We always start by seeking to be clear in our own minds what the biblical standard is that we seek to uphold. The Bible teaches that the desire and practice of any sexual activity outside the covenant relationship of marriage between a man and a woman is wrong in God's sight. Homosexuality is by that definition sinful and is against the command of God but also against the explicit form and clear purpose of male and female bodies. Transgenderism is a rejection of God's creative design and providence. The Bible teaches this both in the Old and the New Testaments. Although one has to be discerning about their use, there are also testimonies of those who are attracted to people of the same sex but seek to be faithful to the Bible's teaching.[4]

First a few guidelines, and then some ideas on what to say.

Be straightforward and honest

Be honest about what the Bible teaches. People can spot evasion tactics a mile off. In 2018 evangelical Christian Tim Farron, former Leader of the Liberal Democrats in the UK, went public with his regret at having given false answers while leader of the party when questioned about his views on homosexuality. It was an embarrassing admission. In 2023 Kate Forbes stood for election to the leadership of the Scottish National Party, during which time she made no secret of her biblical views on homosexuality (and abortion) when asked about them, for which she was widely pilloried. Despite this she came within a hair's-breadth of winning the vote and gained respect for her integrity.

Be compassionate

Before we trot out carelessly our theological position, it is important to recognise that we are talking to real people who may have direct or indirect experience of the issue and your responses might be painful for them. They may be same-sex attracted or struggling with gender dysphoria themselves, or have a close relative affected this way, and our words may come across as hurtful and cruel. So make it clear that you only want the best for others and are genuinely seeking to care. When you say that you love and welcome everyone, make sure you really do mean it and make sure you *sound* like you mean it, or you will just come across as cold and judgmental.

---

4.   See, e.g., 'True Freedom Trust' and 'Living Out'.

Acknowledge that gay people and those in gay relationships are valued members of society and their rights to be free from harassment and harm should be upheld and protected by everyone, especially Christians. We can also affirm that because of God's common grace and our outworking as image bearers there can be good fruit from a wrong relationship. That doesn't make the relationship right, but it cannot be denied.

Bear in mind that the dominant cultural narrative is that to deny someone's self-identity is as unacceptable as racism, so we need to make a special effort for our compassion to be heard. My own experience has been that explaining what I believe calmly and with evident respect for the people I am talking to – and talking about – has a power to it.

Be confident

Christian morality and finding our identity in the people God has made us to be are good things. More broadly, on sexual ethics, the longer I spend in pastoral ministry, the more I realise how good God's design for marriage is. For young people in particular, this may look as if God has placed a jar full of sweets before us but told us we may only have one! But a true perspective is often only obtained when in conversation with those who have gone their own way, stepped outside of God's good plan and are now badly messed up. Then we realise how caring and loving His purposes are for us. Those things taken in defiance of God and which were expected to be sweet have only left a bitter taste and much heartache.

Dealing with the tough questions

So, bearing all the above in mind, how do we begin to respond to those tricky questions about sexuality and identity?

Let's start with the most basic question: Is gay sex sinful?

You can say things like this:

'Any sex outside Christian marriage is not what God wants so, yes, I believe it is not right or good.'

'The practice of any sex outside of marriage goes against God's design and will for us, so it's detrimental and ultimately destructive.'

What about when people say that there are plenty of Christians and churches that accept gay sex and marriage? Such attitudes, almost all of which are limited to the contemporary Western world, are outliers both historically and internationally. It is we who represent the consistent teaching of the church through the ages. So you could say:

'I support the teaching of the Bible, which is the teaching of the majority of churches in the world and throughout history, that sex is a great gift from God to be enjoyed within marriage between a man and a woman. This is also the view across most of the major world religions. This view is nothing new or unusual.'

We may be accused of being unloving. Deal with this by explaining how we may best love others:

'God calls me to love other people and I honestly believe the best way to do so is to tell them the truth and to encourage them to do the right thing. Loving people doesn't mean affirming them whatever they do, especially when it is self-destructive. The most loving thing I can do is be honest about what is best for them. Even if it requires sacrifice, it is always better in the end to go God's way.'

Here is what might seem a slightly obscure question, only for Bible scholars, but I have heard many non-Christians in private conversations or in debates in the media ask a version of this one:

'We don't ban prawns and stone adulterers so why ban sex with other people of the same sex?'

The question is picking up on the fact that in the Old Testament laws given to Moses and God's people Israel, many things were banned and the punishments were severe. They can point out that we clearly are not obeying all the Old Testament laws such as not eating shellfish (Lev. 11:10) or meting out capital punishment for adulterers (Lev. 20:10-12).

This is a complex issue, which needs more than a few sentences to fully answer, but often we have to give something of an answer and I suggest we could say something like this:

'The very specific food laws and some other aspects of the Old Testament Jewish legal system were part of the law for God's people as a nation before the coming of Jesus Christ. Jesus and the apostles clearly explain, that these laws no longer apply.[5] Israel is no longer required to keep itself separate from other people and no nation is under the direct rule of God. However, the rules on sexual morality and marriage are set before the Old Testament Law, at creation, and then re-stated in the New Testament so they are not on the same category as food laws, or the judicial system.'

Some people might say to you:

'It was just the Old Testament and the Apostle Paul that condemned homosexuality. Jesus didn't.'

You might reply:

'In His teaching Jesus clearly upholds the Old Testament's teaching on sex, and even strengthens it in some ways (see Matt. 5:27-32 on adultery and divorce). He also quotes from Genesis 1 and 2 (in Matt. 19:4-5) in which God makes human beings as male and female and brings them together as man and wife into the

---

5. See, e.g., Mark 7:19; Acts 10; Acts 15:1-29.

marriage relationship (see Gen. 1:27 and Gen. 2:24). The implication is clear: that Jesus did not see homosexual acts and relationships as being consistent with God's purpose in creating men and women for a sexual intimacy with each other.

'Secondly, the Christian faith treats the whole of the Bible as God's Word to us. It is not for us to pick and choose what we like or don't like. If Moses or Paul says something, it is for us to accept it as from God, just as we do the words of Jesus.'

Another typical question is:

'What would you do if your child told you he or she were gay?'

My own response would be:

'I would continue to love them, as always. And because I love them, I would show them what the Bible teaches and remind them that this is ultimately best for them.'

You might be asked:

'Why don't you keep your moral judgments to yourself?'

You could respond:

'You are not keeping your moral judgments to yourself when you judge me for being anti-gay. Why should you be free to do what you say and I am not?'

A popular question is:

'Did God make me gay?'

You could reply:

'No one really knows why people become attracted to the same sex. There seems to be no biological reason, but perhaps it is a combination of predisposition plus the experiences we go through, especially as a child. Also, when our culture affirms and praises some feelings and practices, it can lead to a copycat mentality and developing habits. In a broken world we can end up thinking and behaving in ways that are wrong and destructive, but we cannot assume that God made us that way.'

Writing on the 'Answers in Genesis'[6] website, Dr Georgia Purdom states that:

> From an evolutionary perspective, it really wouldn't make any sense for homosexuality to have a biological basis. One of the major tenets of evolution is reproduction and passing on one's genes to the next generation. Both past and present scientific studies have shown no conclusive evidence that homosexual behaviour is biological; and even if there is a biological basis, the researchers themselves admit that it would likely make a relatively small contribution.

You could also ask some questions of your own:

'Just as a thought exercise, if God exists, would it be OK for Him to set the rules about sex and relationships?'

Most people will not answer a simple 'no' to this question. They will most likely answer with a qualified 'yes', and then you are into a discussion: we can talk about the evidence for God, or about the authority and ownership of a creator, or about the fact they agree it is OK for God to set the rules, but they don't like the rules, or our interpretation of those rules. Whatever route they take, you have plenty to talk about now!

'What kind of sexual relationships are acceptable to you? Are there any that are not? How did you reach these conclusions?'

Asking what is the moral framework for evaluating relationships is useful. Someone might say that it only matters if two people love each other, or that they consent to sex. Almost everyone will draw the line somewhere, often to do with children, but it can be good to get them to consider why they drew the line there. You may still end up disagreeing, but at least you are now agreeing that

---

6. https://answersingenesis.org/blogs/georgia-purdom/2019/01/14/biology-gender-sexuality/

the difference is about the moral code and you can argue for the authority and goodness of the one in the Bible.

'Do you think any combination of adults and children is appropriate for a healthy family? How did you decide this?'

This question gets people talking about families. Again, there are exceptions but most people think families are a good thing and they instinctively know that stable relationships, and generally between two heterosexual parents, are the healthiest for children. But even if they think any combination is fine they will probably need to say that love and respect need to be there.

Piers Morgan interviewed the actor Kirk Cameron on CNN's *Piers Morgan Tonight* in 2012.[7] I recently stumbled across their conversation and was impressed with the calmness and clarity of Cameron's responses to Morgan's questions. As a bonus, he also does a great job answering questions about abortion. I thought they were worth including:

PM: Do you think homosexuality is a sin?

KC: I think that it's… it's unnatural. I think that it's… it's detrimental and ultimately destructive to so many of the foundations of civilisation.

PM: What do you do if one of your six kids says, 'Dad, bad news, I'm gay.'

KC: I'd sit down and have a heart-to-heart with them just like you would with your kids.

PM: If one of my sons said that, I'd say, 'That's great, son. As long as you're happy.' What would you say?

KC: Well, I wouldn't say, 'That's great, son, as long as you're happy.' I'm going to say, you know, 'There's all sorts of issues that we need to wrestle through in our life. Just because you feel one way doesn't mean we should act on everything that we feel.'

---

7.   https://youtu.be/JhGQUKoH_TE

PM: I'm making the point that seven states in America have now legalised gay marriage.

KC: Well, Piers, you're speaking to a man who's a Christian and I believe that all of us are sinful. I could stand at the top of the list and say that I need a saviour and I need an overhaul of the heart more than anyone. And so that's what I teach my kids. I teach them the values that I hold dear. I treasure the God that loves me and forgives me of my sin. I would teach that to my children, as well as having a wonderful relationship with them that my wife and I work on every single day. So your value system, my value system, we're all going to pick a standard against which we judge behaviour morally. All of our laws ultimately, at their core, are going to be based on a moral evaluation.

PM: So what's your view of abortion?

KC: I think that it's wrong.

PM: Under any circumstances?

KC: Under any circumstances.

PM: Even rape and incest?

KC: I think someone who is ultimately willing to murder a child, even to fix another tragic end, a devastating situation like rape or incest or things like that, is not taking the moral high road. I think that we're compounding the problem by also murdering a little child.

PM: Could you honestly look a daughter in the eye if she was raped and say you have got to have that child?

KC: Yes, and 'I will help you'.

PM: You would do that?

KC: Yes, of course.

PM: I find that amazing that people would say that.

KC: Because I love my daughter. I love that little child. This is a little creature made in God's image. Perhaps – imagine if you were the result of that and you had been aborted. We wouldn't be here having this conversation. So I value life above all things.

You can kind of get the feel of the conversation from the transcript but if you watch it, you can see how challenging these questions are, both personally and intellectually. What Kirk Cameron manages really well is to answer the questions in a direct way that just seems authentic and sincere.

Is God good?

Definitely up there as the top question we get asked in any evangelistic conversation, Bible study, or media debate is 'Why does God allow suffering?' Let's be honest – it's also one of the top questions that we as Christians often ask God and each other as well.

Why are there illnesses, disasters, premature death, and evil people who are allowed to do terrible things? Either God is so weak He just can't prevent it, or He just doesn't care, or He is cruel and vindictive – or more likely God's not there at all.

Before answering the question, we need to figure out the context. Why is the questioner asking? Is it borne out of sincere curiosity, maybe bitter experience or just a desire to shut down any debate. They may use this as their knock-out punch for Christians, or they may be going through the horrible experience of a miscarriage or the death of a loved one. We need to be sensitive to that in the way we answer.

This is not an easy question to answer in a few words. Sometimes it is best to simply say:

'I don't know why God has allowed this, but I know He is good and just and one day it will all make sense.'

But there are other things we can say such as:

'Suffering happens because the world was broken by the sin of Adam and Eve and ever since there has been sickness, death, fighting, and wars.' (Gen. 3, Rom. 8:22).

'In a fallen world people do not behave well all the time so there are often direct human causes of suffering; a person does something bad to someone else or there is a natural consequence of an individual's lifestyle, or the outworking of war, greed, oppression, industrialisation, overpopulation, and so on.'

'Jesus went through much worse suffering, with a good cause in mind. His suffering was not meaningless, and did not demonstrate God's weakness, malevolence, or non-existence but rather His power, love, and presence. I know God is good because He reached out to us like this, even though we didn't deserve it.'

'I can't explain suffering but the Christian faith can give you hope in the suffering and beyond it.'

'The very fact that you feel outrage about the world's suffering assumes a moral universe and that there is such a thing as good and evil. You know it. It's because God has made us morally accountable and morally sensible. This cannot be explained with a closed, mechanical view of the universe in which God doesn't exist. If you assume there are such things as right and wrong, good and evil, you need to be able to explain why, and you cannot do it without reference to a higher authority from whom such standards derive – God.'

Depending on how much time you have it might be useful to explore these ideas:

'Some Christians argue that if God had created a world in which no one could choose to sin of their own free will – and thus there would never be human suffering – it would not actually be a world worth living in. We would just be automatons, robots. What sort of a perfect world would that be? That's worth pondering.'

'God is absolutely sovereign – in control – of all things, but never acts in such a way that human responsibility is removed or minimised. Humans are responsible for their actions.'

'It is important to say that the universe operates for the glory of God, not for our pleasure. His character defines what is good. And His great love and care for us are seen most clearly in what Jesus does in living and dying for us.'

'Why does evil exist? I cannot tell you why, but I know that there must be a sufficient and good reason for it in the purposes of God. With our limited perspective, we cannot possibly locate and compute all the interlocking events – their causes and consequences – that ultimately bring about the good and loving plan of God. We see just a small part of what He is doing, and so we must trust Him for the rest.'

'Because we know from the Bible that God is absolutely good we know also that there is a reason for every seemingly meaningless moment of suffering. If He were to explain it all to us now, it is highly likely that we would not fully understand it, because He is so far above us, and His wisdom and understanding so much greater than ours.'

'Suffering is not significant compared to eternity.' (Rom. 8:18)

'We often learn through bad experience and we teach or comfort others by having been through troubles that they are now experiencing.' (2 Cor. 1:3-4)

The reliability of the Bible

Most people we talk to are not liberal scholars who cast doubts on the authorship, dating or authenticity of Bible books or question the reality of miracles or prophecies. They are more likely to say, 'I don't really care what the Bible says; it is not relevant to me.'

However, some might say, 'The Bible is full of errors' or 'The Bible is just a collection of mythological tales passed down by word of mouth', or 'You don't really believe in the resurrection and miracles of Jesus, do you?'

It's therefore good to have some responses ready on the reliability and the relevance of the Bible. A great thing to establish at the outset is to say:

'What we have is what was written by eyewitnesses of the time. You may believe it or not, but it's what the writers saw and heard.'

'We do not have the original manuscripts of the Bible texts, but they were copied by people who gave meticulous attention to detail. This copying method was so careful and precise that the New Testament alone is considered to be 99.5 per cent textually pure. This means that of the 6,000 Greek copies (the New Testament was written in Greek), and the additional 21,000 copies in other languages, the content varies by only one-half of 1 per cent. Of this very small number, the great majority of the variants are easily corrected by comparing them to other copies that don't have the 'typos' or by simply reading the context. The differences are very minor. None of them affect major doctrinal truth and the words and deeds of Christ are reliably transmitted to us.'

'The Bible is so exceedingly accurate in its transmission from the originals to the present copies, that if you compare it to any other ancient writing, the Bible is light years ahead in terms of the number of manuscripts and accuracy. If the Bible were to be discredited as being unreliable, then it would be necessary to discard the writings of Homer, Plato, and Aristotle as also unreliable since they are far, far less well preserved than the Bible.'[8]

---

8. https://carm.org/christianity/is-the-bible-reliable/ *Accessed 4 May 2023.*

'The New Testament was written by those who either knew Jesus personally or were under the direction of those who did. They wrote what they saw and heard. They wrote about the resurrection of Christ. They recorded His miracles and His sayings. This is what we have. We can debate whether we believe it, but we can't pretend it is an unreliable record of what the authors wrote down.'

Another useful approach is to comment on the Bible's coherence and internal consistency. Here is a book which brings together texts written by about forty different authors, over a period of 1,500 years, most of whom didn't know each other. They wrote in three languages (Hebrew, Aramaic, and Greek) from vastly different cultural backgrounds. And yet, taken as a whole, there is a remarkable unity to the overall message that becomes ever clearer the more it is studied. Think about the classic murder mystery drama, and how the different threads of the story all come together as the action unfolds. That is a relatively simple drama, written by a single author with a clear purpose in mind in organising and developing the tale. We marvel at the skill of a good novelist to bring all the subplots together to a believable and satisfying conclusion. But compare that feat with the seeming impossibility of compiling a book by multiple authors over a millennium and a half, containing such diverse elements as history, poetry, biography, and letters, and yet with one consistent and united meaning. That is the astonishing, supernatural nature of the Bible – a book written by human authors but inspired and overseen by God.

We can also talk about how other historical sources back up the biblical record. The Bible itself is a historical record of great significance for historians, but extra-biblical sources also support its content. So we might talk about the Hittites:

'Sceptics used to criticise the Bible for referring to the Hittite people because, prior to 1876, there was no archaeological or other evidence that any such culture ever existed. Then in that year such proof began to come to light, and by the early twentieth century the vastness of the Hittite nation and its influence in the ancient world had become accepted fact.'[9]

At one time other historical figures such as King David or the Roman governor Pilate were unknown outside the Bible, but later discoveries eventually confirmed the biblical evidence.

The fulfilment of prophecy is another avenue worth exploring. Various biblical characters looked forward to future events, sometimes centuries ahead. If even just one of these had been realised, it would be astounding, but it happened many, many times over. Some of the prophecies were fulfilled in a short amount of time (Abraham and Sarah had a son in old age, Peter denied Jesus three times, Paul was a witness for Jesus in Rome, etc.). Others were realised hundreds of years later. The Old Testament contains, it is estimated, some *three hundred* messianic prophecies that were fulfilled by the coming of Jesus, His life, death, and resurrection. The odds on these all coming to fruition in the life of one person are vanishingly small. The only reasonable explanation is that a supernatural power and wisdom was inspiring the words of the prophets.[10]

Meaning, purpose, hope, and the hiddenness of God

It might seem surprising that the 'hiddenness of God' should be a popular issue raised by non-Christians but this was confirmed to me by someone who meets such

9. https://www.gotquestions.org/why-should-I-believe-the-Bible.html
10. ibid.

people all over the country. As I reflected on it I could see why.

The complaint voiced by many is that although they are genuine seekers for meaning and purpose and want to know if God is there, they have been unable to find Him. This silence thus invites the conclusion that He does not exist. Surely, they argue, if God is loving and wants a relationship with us, He would help us in our search and provide enough compelling evidence to conclude that He is there. So, they conclude, either God doesn't exist or, if He does, He is vindictive and cruel to ignore their heartfelt inquiries.

In his recent book, *The God Desire*,[11] comedian David Baddiel argues that the almost universal longing for God within humanity is just a projection of our own hopes and fears. He concludes that the intensity of our wish for God to exist is, in fact, strong evidence that He does not. We are all afraid of oblivion and this leads us to indulge in the fantasy of a divine being who will rescue us from death. He says he would love to believe, but that he cannot bring himself to do so because 'there is no evidence to support the existence of God'.

How should we respond to these arguments?

Firstly, we need to challenge the assumption that a search for God is unhindered by any fault or lack on our part. Are we capable of relating personally to God if we simply desire to do so?

So we might say:

'It is a false premise that people are genuinely predisposed to believe and open to a relationship with God. In Genesis 3 we see Adam and Eve hiding from God when He came looking for them. Ever since, we have been hiding too, even when we say that we are really seeking Him. The Bible teaches that by nature we are hostile to

---

11. Baddiel, David, *The God Desire* (TLS Books, 2023).

God – we have rebelled against Him. We are morally compromised, and having a curiosity to know whether God exists is not the same as wanting to acknowledge Him as our leader, and thus being subject to His righteous direction for our lives.'

'If I could give you undeniable proof that God exists and wants a relationship with you, in which you willingly give up control of your life to Him, would you believe? The fact is that the problem is not so much one of lack of evidence, but a lack of a humble heart willing to submit to God. You are not as open as you think you are.'

'God is not hidden; He has revealed Himself in Jesus. Let me tell you some more about Him…'

Historical injustices and the church

Our society in general, and young people in particular have a real sensitivity about justice. They often point the finger at the church for historic injustices including slavery, anti-Semitism and the exploitation of the poor and women. They can also point to more recent abuse scandals in the church. What should we say?

'It is right that we should humbly accept that such abuses were carried out in the name of Christ by His church. There have been many times when Christians have not acted in the way Jesus would want us to, when on earth, He always displayed perfect love and justice in all His dealings with people. We have sinned, and still sin, when we fail to live as He lived. It is important that we own up to this. In the end we need to judge Christianity by the teachings and by the central character of Jesus Christ who always acted with perfect love and justice.'

But we should also bring some historical perspective to this discussion:

'Some practices that we now, rightly, condemn, need to be seen in light of the cultural norms of their day. They were widely practised and accepted by most people and were not peculiar to Christians. That doesn't make them right, then, or now, but it does give another angle on what happened. And there are things that take place in our day which, we sincerely hope and trust, future generations will look on as barbaric, including abortion and child mutilation for transgender purposes.'

What about other religions?

A religion is 'a set of beliefs concerning the cause, nature, and purpose of the universe, especially when considered as the creation of a superhuman agency or agencies, usually involving devotional and ritual observances, and often containing a moral code governing the conduct of human affairs.'[12]

Is Christianity really all that special? Isn't it just another religion?

Christianity is like other religions in that it teaches about a divine being and how to worship Him, and it advocates a moral code. But it is fundamentally different from all other faiths in various very significant ways:

a. Its claims are founded upon detailed historical records provided by eyewitness accounts that can be verified by external evidence (1 John 1:1; 2 Pet. 1:16; Luke 1:1-4).

b. It introduces a unique person, Jesus Christ, who claimed to be the Son of God, whose words have a power and authority that have captivated people down the centuries to the present day.

c. In some way or another, every religion requires us to earn our acceptance with its deity. Christianity is very different. Peace with God is received on the strength of His grace – it is His free gift. Instead of us striving

---

12.   https://www.britannica.com/topic/religion. Accessed 12 December 2023.

to reach up to Him, God has reached down to rescue us in the person of Jesus Christ.

Why are there other religions?

Dan Strange provides a concise theological definition of non-Christian religions – they are 'sovereignly directed, variegated and dynamic, collective human idolatrous responses to divine revelation behind which stand deceiving demonic forces. Being antithetically against yet parasitically dependent upon the truth of the Christian worldview, non-Christian religions are "subversively fulfilled" in the gospel of Jesus Christ.'[13] That is excellent for us Christians but not really suitable to answer a sincere enquirer with no Christian background. Something along these lines might be more suitable:

'Humans are persistently religious beings. In every age and culture, people have had an instinct that some higher being (or beings) exists whom we ought to worship. This is not to be wondered at if we accept that, as Genesis tells us, we have all been made in the image of God as His special creation. Therefore, we all carry about within us a residual sense of who we were created to be, the reality of which has been lost through our rebellion and fall. All other religions are thus attempts to recover that relationship with the divine, but doing so using human wisdom and ingenuity, rather than seeking God's own remedy which is found in the Bible. These efforts necessarily distort the faith and worship which is described there and which God Himself prescribes for us to follow.'

Some people will argue that nevertheless all religions ultimately lead us to the truth whichever one is followed. But the exclusive claims of the Bible, especially from the mouth of Jesus Himself, make it impossible to lump

---

13. Strange, Dan, *For their rock is not our rock* (Apollos, 2014), p. 46

Christianity in with other faiths. He is either the only way to God or He is no Saviour at all.

Those who complain that such exclusive claims are arrogant do so from an implied position of superiority, claiming to be able to judge better than anyone else what is true. What gives them that right? Doesn't that display the very arrogance they claim to reject?

Religion is just about where you were born

Some say if you were born in Morocco, you would almost certainly grow up believing Islam to be the true faith. In other words, one's religion is an accident of birth and nothing at all to do with whether it is actually true or not; you were born in the UK, and had some Christian influence, therefore you are a Christian. But that fact doesn't prove whether one religion is true or not. If you were born in Morocco, you wouldn't be a religious pluralist or an atheist. It's just not fair to say, 'All claims about religions are historically conditioned except the one I'm making just now.' Moreover, a follower of Jesus does not blindly accept the faith of his family or culture – it is a personal relationship with God, freely entered into, based on the authority of the biblical record. It is always useful to study the claims of other religions, and having done so, we find (as described above) the uniqueness of Christianity sets it far apart from the rest.

Science and evolution disprove the idea of God as creator

There is an assumption (unjustified as it happens) that science has settled the fact that our world and the universe is very old and that it came about by chance over a very long period of time, with no supreme, creative mind behind it all.

However, we need to challenge that view, which is often held in a very unthinking way by those who have never really looked into the matter and who often hold this view at the same time as believing in some kind of transcendent spiritual world, up there or out there.

There are plenty of things we can say to make people stop and consider again. Here are a few:

The world looks designed, so there must be a designer

Examples of apparent evidence of a designer's handiwork can be seen from the smallest cell to the biggest galaxy. There is astonishing complexity and order in every part of our world, from the way bees make honey, to the functioning of the octopus or elephant, from the intricate operations going on in every single cell to the organisation of the human brain. It defies comprehension that all of these impossibly complex structures and functions could have come about by pure chance.

There is so much information in the world

DNA contains all the genetic information required to make us who we are. If you stretched out a strand of DNA in just one cell of the human body, it would be about two metres long. But if you extended all the DNA in all your cells together they would reach to the moon and back about 150,000 times! That gives you some idea of the complexity. To put it another way it is about 1GB of data. All sensible information. There are no examples of information of this complexity and scale being spontaneously created from nothing. Can we really believe that random processes have created all this? As a counter argument to the evolutionary theory that information evolved, apart from this being hopelessly unlikely, evidence from genetics clearly shows that mutations, rather than creating new and ever-more complex DNA as required by evolution, cause continuous degradation of DNA. Geneticist, Dr John Sanford, calls this genetic entropy and it eventually causes extinction.[14]

The universe is finely tuned

Our universe is so precisely fine-tuned that life on earth would be impossible if anything was changed by even microscopic amounts. For example, the earth is 93 million miles from the sun. If this distance increased by just 1 per cent the earth would become a frozen waste. If the earth was 5 per cent closer to the sun the seas would turn to steam and there could be no life.

The earth is tilted at 23 degrees to produce our seasons by changing the amount and degree of sunlight. If the angle were different, water vapour from the oceans would move north and south and the earth would gradually be encased by an icecap.

If the crust of the earth were only ten feet thicker, there would be no oxygen and all animal life would die.

Added to this, there are a number of mathematical constants which we don't generally talk about; the strength of gravity when measured against the strength of electromagnetism; the strong nuclear force, and the difference between the masses of the two lightest quarks. It's OK, you don't have to understand or explain these, but just to say that without these precise numbers our life in the universe would not be happening.

The probability of getting all these numbers right by chance is infinitesimally small. Therefore, it seems reasonable to consider that a creative mind lies behind it.

Mathematics works

The precision and regularity of mathematical laws that govern the universe are incredibly complex and sophisticated. Mathematics is often said to be beautiful

---

14. https://www.premierchristianity.com/features/why-im-finally-a-young-earth-creationist/5327.article *Accessed 1 September 2023.*

or elegant, and to contain 'truth' or 'objectivity'. This is another aspect of the natural world that hints at an intelligence behind everything that we see. The more we study the way in which mathematics can be used to describe the order and wonder of creation, the more we find ourselves drawn to the idea of a creator.

There has to be a first cause

(This is usually called the 'cosmological argument'.)

The reasoning goes like this:

Everything that exists has been caused by something, which has itself been caused by something else. The further backwards in time that we go, the more steps of cause and effect we will find. But unless the universe has always existed (which scientists do not believe), there must have been a 'first cause' – something that was not itself brought into existence by some prior event or power. Where did this uncreated 'thing' come from? What could it be? Many theologians and philosophers conclude that it must be an eternal, divine being, existing independently of anything else and the source of all other matter.

The moral argument

This argument has been presented in different forms by various philosophers throughout history, but the basic idea is the fact that a shared sense of morality among human beings cannot be adequately explained without reference to an external source of those moral codes.

The best explanation for this phenomenon is the existence of a God from whom such objective morality derives. Naturalism and atheism do not provide adequate alternative explanations.

One version of this argument is attributed to the philosopher Immanuel Kant (1724–1804), who argued that moral obligations are grounded in the existence of a necessary being – a god.

Human consciousness

The mysterious and wonderful thing that humans possess which we refer to as 'consciousness' cannot be adequately explained by the physical mechanisms of the human body and brain. This suggests that there is a non-material aspect to our existence. That something exists right there within us which seems to transcend the physical world, is another strong indicator that it is foolish to imagine our world – and the universe – as simply a meaningless jumble of atoms. At our very heart we all carry about within us the stamp of a creative being outside of ourselves.

The resurrection of Jesus Christ

Taking a different approach completely, we may say that the biblical record of Jesus' resurrection forms part of the evidence for the existence of God. Many eyewitness accounts reported the death, and then, three days later, the return to life of Jesus of Nazareth. Desperate as they were to prove it otherwise, neither the Romans nor the Jewish leaders could provide any evidence to the contrary. Those early Christians were so convinced of His resurrection that they were willing to die as martyrs for that belief; they knew it had happened.

This supernatural intervention into the natural way of things – dead men don't rise again – is just one of very many indications that God has given us of His existence. All we can see is not all that there is!

Counter-arguments against evolution

There are good arguments which more directly enter enemy territory and deploy scientific arguments against evolution. It can be useful to point out things such as:

- The lack of fossils showing evolution between species,

- The presence of soft tissue in dinosaur bones that clearly indicates these bones cannot be millions of years old, since biological tissue disintegrates rapidly,

- The presence of radioactive carbon in samples from essentially every layer in the geological column clearly indicates that these layers are not hundreds of millions of years old, because after 90,000 years (at most) radiocarbon would be undetectable.[15]

You can add to this list with some basic online research, but scientific counter-arguments need to be deployed carefully and not fully relied on. It is best to use them to raise questions and sow some seeds of doubt about the scientific method, not to shoot for totally disproving the evolutionary model.

So be ready

I used to spend some Fridays visiting a nearby town to debate with Muslims on the streets and in a mosque. What I found immensely challenging was the confidence they had that they were right. They would sometimes say to me, 'Why do you keep saying that this is what Christians believe, or I think this or that? Why don't you just say that it is the truth?' It was a good point.

Jesus is Lord. So be confident. Be ready to argue for the beauty and truth of the gospel. Be aware of the hostility we will probably face, but enthusiastic about the opportunities.

We stand on solid ground as we give reasons for our hope, based on the credibility of the witness of the Scriptures. It is not our truth; it is *the* truth.

In the marketplace of ideas, this is truth for sharing.

---

15. ibid.

Questions for reflection and discussion

1. Do you find it easy to talk about things to do with your faith? Why or why not? Do you pray for opportunities to speak? Pray about it now!

2. What is the hardest question you get asked or would worry about being asked in a public setting. How could you prepare for that line of questioning?

3. What do you think are the most compelling reasons to believe the gospel? Could you summarise each of them in just a few sentences?

Chapter 3
Market Streets

'Out in the open wisdom calls aloud,
she raises her voice in the public square;
on top of the wall she cries out,
at the city gate she makes her speech.'
(Proverbs 1:20-21)

*'So go to the street corners
and invite to the banquet anyone you find.'*
(Matthew 22:9)

Stephen Lungu grew up in a black township near Salisbury, in what was then Rhodesia (now Zimbabwe). He was practically abandoned by his family and started sleeping under a bridge and scavenging food from rich white people's dustbins. Soon he was recruited into a revolutionary gang called the Black Shadows. When a travelling evangelist came to town, Stephen was sent to firebomb the event, carrying his bag of bombs and mingling with the crowd. Instead of throwing bombs he stayed to listen to the preacher and in a most remarkable demonstration of the power of the Holy Spirit, he became a Christian right there and then.

The next day he started preaching on buses and, in between bus rides, he would 'take up a place in the market and preach from there'.[1] At this point he didn't own a Bible and anyway he couldn't read. He had less Bible knowledge than most infants in your church pre-school group. He hardly knew what to tell people to do if they wanted to follow Jesus. But as a result of almost his first sermon on a bus people were converted, some of whom became church pastors and are still in ministry forty years later. Lungu's heartfelt desire was to tell people about his Saviour, and so he went where the people were. He was converted by what might be called a traditional evangelistic event, albeit the reason for him attending was to be a saboteur rather than a conventional seeker.

But what he then did was pretty unconventional even by the cultural standards of the time. He wasn't part of any church's evangelistic programme and because of his background he didn't have conventional social connections. He just reasoned that he needed to go where people were and tell them the gospel. So he went into a public place and spoke to whoever would listen. And they did listen. Would you be willing to go public in that way?

You might say in response that this was an exceptional work of the Holy Spirit operating through an extraordinary individual, so not necessarily repeatable. You could also say, as we have already discussed in previous chapters, that our marketplace could take the form of many different physical or virtual locations. So you might conclude that we don't need to, like Paul, do our reasoning in a literal marketplace.

But is that really true? Is the real reason that we hesitate because we are not brave enough, or enthusiastic enough about the gospel? Some days I wonder.

In the rest of this book I want to consider how we might engage with the various manifestations of our

---

1. Lungu, Stephen with Coomes, Anne, *Out of the Black Shadows* (10Publishing, 2020), p. 120

contemporary marketplace. In this chapter we will look at one possible example of 'going out to where people are': public, street-level evangelism.

Street preaching

Maybe you have heard that collective groan when a busker gets on your underground (subway) train. Everyone looks down even more intensely at their phone or book as the performance begins. Your unwanted entertainer's jolly manner does nothing to endear you; you just want it to end. A street preacher provokes even more embarrassment and resentment, and it is surely therefore no wonder that so many of us feel great awkwardness and even horror at the thought of doing the same.

I remember being on holiday and walking around Padstow harbour in Cornwall, England and coming across a man with a Bible verse on a placard, making an intrusive noise through a battered old loudspeaker. He was being faithful to the gospel message but no one was really listening; he wasn't offering henna tattoos, hair-braiding, or ice-cream. I understand why people ignored him and, to be honest, until I began researching for this book, I was pretty sceptical about any kind of unsolicited public preaching. I had done it a few times and I didn't wish to repeat the exercise. It was an ordeal, a feat of endurance, and it felt insincere and unreal.

I admit that it is not everyone's gift or calling and maybe it isn't culturally appropriate in the UK today in the same way it was in first-century Athens or eighteenth-century Britain – or Rhodesia in the 1960s. But there is something about it that I can't quite simply dismiss as an anachronism – something from the past that should remain there. So please stick with me for this chapter, even if you are as sceptical as I was, and let's see where we all end up.

The biblical record

As we have already seen, we don't know exactly how Paul would have gone about his reasoning in the marketplace. Would he have stood or sat around and waited for people to come up and start talking to him? Would he have taken the initiative and approached them to open a conversation? Or might he have just started preaching to the passers-by? Did he call out in a loud voice as a crowd slowly gathered? It's certainly possible. Street preaching has an impressive pedigree:

Many of the Old Testament prophets proclaimed their message in the open air, not within walls or other formal settings. Sometimes these were organised gatherings of God's people, meeting outside because of the sheer numbers involved. The Middle Eastern climate – warm and dry – would normally have made such gatherings more natural, although one notable exception was the fascinating account in post-exilic Jerusalem when Ezra gathered the people together to castigate them for intermarriage with non-Jews. We read in Ezra 10:9 that the people were 'greatly distressed by the occasion and because of the rain'. (They should try living here in the UK!)

But Old Testament proclamation wasn't always to those who had gathered outside to listen to God's Word. Jonah walked the streets of Nineveh proclaiming, 'Forty more days and Nineveh will be overthrown' (Jonah 3:4). I don't think it was a series of meetings; I get the impression he travelled across the city telling people in the streets that judgment was coming. It worked, and the people repented, even though Jonah had been a very reluctant preacher.

68

Isaiah was given a message by God for his people and was instructed to, 'Shout it aloud, do not hold back. Raise your voice like a trumpet. Declare to my people their rebellion and to the descendants of Jacob their sins' (Isa. 58:1). This sounds as if he was being told to proclaim the message on the streets rather than have an informal chat or give a dry lecture.

Jeremiah also received a prophetic commission from God, but there is no record of formal meetings, whether indoors or out, but he is called to 'cry aloud' in Jerusalem (Jer. 2:2; 4:5). He also taught in the temple courts, which were public spaces (Jer. 26:2), and on one occasion he employs a spokesperson, Baruch, to read his words at the entrance to thc temple (Jer. 36:8), for which they both get into a lot of trouble.

Ezekiel was told by God to prophesy the coming siege of Jerusalem with not just words but also what we might call visual aids (e.g., Ezek. 4:3). It included elements of 'street drama', lying down for long periods of time and cutting his hair and beard, weighing it on scales and throwing some of it into the wind (Ezek. 5:1-4).

This sort of public street level proclamation was most probably the main delivery method for all the major and minor prophets in the Old Testament. What they first spoke out to the people where they gathered, we now have recorded as written documents in Scripture.

The last and greatest prophet before Christ was John the Baptist who preached in the wilderness and the area around the Jordan River (Matt. 3:1-2; Mark 1:4; Luke 3:3). This seems very much like open-air preaching – and all a bit spontaneous – to me!

When we come to our great teacher and example Jesus, He uses all possible means to deliver His message. He often taught in the synagogues (Matt. 9:35; Luke 4:16-21; Mark 1:21-28) but His famous 'Sermon on the Mount' (Matt. 5-7) was outside, spoken to a semi-formal gathering. He also taught His disciples at length while outside on the Mount of Olives, just before His trial and execution (Matt. 24-25). He also taught the crowds in the public square setting of the temple courts (John 7:14). These spaces were a place where all kinds of people could gather (including Gentiles in the outer court). They came there for worship and learning but also to socialise and to debate. In John 7 Jesus engages in what could best be described as open-air preaching when He projects His words through those courts: 'On the last and greatest day of the festival, Jesus stood and said in a loud voice, "Let anyone who is thirsty come to me and drink. Whoever believes in me, as Scripture has said, rivers of living water will flow from within them."' (John 7:37-38).

Outside of those settings, as we read the Gospels, we get the impression that Jesus' ministry included a whole range of speaking scenarios, including informal dialogues, group debates, and many impromptu teaching sessions as people interacted with Him. At times He responded to questions from His disciples by directing His answers to the wider crowd as well (Matt. 11:7). Often there would have been no fixed audience; some people probably drifted into earshot and out again. At other times He might also have dealt with further questions and even heckling (Matt. 12:38; Luke 12:13).

Jesus also sent out His twelve disciples on local mission trips to proclaim the message in town after town (Matt. 10). One assumes that they found public places and started speaking. If they were rejected, they moved on.

Finally, just before He returns to the Father, the risen Jesus gives His followers the Great Commission (Matt. 28) to go into all the world with the good news. Having seen how Jesus Himself ministered, they would surely have understood that their going would take them to many diverse settings, not just the formal environment of a public meeting in a synagogue or other places of worship.

The first time Peter preached the gospel in Acts 2, was immediately after the Holy Spirit fell upon the disciples, as the apostles spilled out onto the streets, and the crowd that gathered heard and understood their words in all their various native languages.

As the church started to grow, so too did opposition from the authorities. In Acts 5 the apostles are arrested and then 'during the night an angel of the Lord opened the doors of the jail and brought them out. "Go, stand in the temple courts," he said, "and tell the people all about this new life."' (Acts 5:19-20).

Throughout the rest of the book of Acts the apostles and other early Christians went about preaching the good news. Sometimes the setting was the local synagogue or lecture theatre but also there were impromptu talks in response to unforeseen circumstances and unexpected opportunities. As Charles Spurgeon said to his preaching students, 'The apostles and their immediate successors delivered their message of mercy not only in their own hired houses and in the synagogues but also anywhere and everywhere as occasion served them.'[2]

And then of course we come back to Paul in the Athens marketplace. He had preached to the Jewish population of the city in their synagogue, but the vast majority of the local people, non-Jews, were elsewhere. So Paul went to where they were – in the streets and in the marketplaces, to where they gathered and discussed and debated. He wasn't invited to speak to them but he did it anyway, and it was as a result of these conversations that he received the invitation to address the Areopagus (Acts 17).

This has been a very brief survey of how, in the Bible, God used human instruments to convey His Word to

---

2. Spurgeon, Charles, *Lectures to my Students* (various editions), p. 235

men and women. But I think it is very clear from the evidence that time and again, over many centuries and in many different cultures and settings, God's messengers went *outdoors*, to where the people were – people who might not at first have been interested, some of whom were hostile. But God used their words and many lives were changed.

Shouldn't it make you ask why most churches don't do it any more?

Church history

The early church met in homes and other public places. Even after 300 years there were still very few church buildings as we would recognise them today. Dedicated meeting places only really started being built in the early fourth century after Christianity was made legal by the Roman Emperor Constantine.

Impressive church buildings were commissioned across the Roman empire, but that did not mean that the only preaching happened 'in church' from then on. Over the centuries, at times and seasons of renewal and restoration, preaching often took place outdoors, away from the established church and their buildings.

In the fourteenth century in Britain, John Wycliffe became the first person to translate the Bible into English from Latin. His followers became known as Lollards, and travelled throughout England preaching in the streets and marketplaces against what they saw as the errors of the Catholic Church.

As part of the bigger Reformation story, the Church of Scotland, a Presbyterian Church was founded by John Knox in the sixteenth century. Amusing sidebar: Knox started out as a bodyguard for a street preacher named George Wishart. (Perhaps every preacher should begin their training as a bodyguard or a club bouncer!) Due to his 'heretical' doctrines, Wishart had not been allowed to preach in church buildings and so went instead into the marketplaces and fields. After Wishart was martyred in 1546, Knox took over as leader of the Scottish Reformation.

William Carey (1761–1834) was a missionary to India and is often referred to as the founder of the modern missionary movement because of the significant influence in his day of an essay he wrote entitled 'An enquiry into the obligations of Christians to use means for the conversion of heathens'. In this he argued that the Great Commission of Matthew 28 remains binding on Christians.[3] He also compiled statistics on religion for every country in the world. Carey worked as a weaver and shoemaker and, despite having had little formal education, taught himself science and languages, going on to translate the Bible into eleven languages.

When he went to India he started by preaching to large crowds that gathered in the streets of the red-light district. One of his converts was a young British sailor named Robert Flockhart (1778–1857), who went back to the British Isles and preached in the streets of Edinburgh for forty-three years until his death. One of Carey's associates, John Chamberlain, would go to the River Ganges where Hindus gathered, and start an argument with one of the Brahmins, the Hindu priests. When the argument drew a crowd, he would preach to those assembled.

John Wesley and George Whitefield were major figures in the Evangelical Revival in Britain and the Great Awakening in America during the eighteenth century. Wesley eventually became a great itinerant evangelist, preaching in the open air to vast crowds, but only after being urged by Whitefield to follow his own example. He had been initially very reluctant to take such a bold

---

3.   Carey, William, *An enquiry into the obligations of Christians* (Carey Kingsgate Press, 1961).

step. He wrote in his journal in 1739: 'In the evening I reached Bristol and met Mr. Whitfield there. I could scarce reconcile myself at first to this strange way of preaching in the fields, of which he set me an example on Sunday, having been all my life (till very lately) so tenacious of every point relating to decency and order that I should have thought the saving of souls almost a sin if it had not been done in a church...'[4]

Whitefield had gone to Bristol having heard of the spiritual, moral and economic plight of the coal miners of nearby Kingswood. These kinds of people were completely beyond the reach of the churches. He thus believed that they could only be reached in the open air. So Whitefield famously preached to them as they came up out of the mines, their faces blackened with coal dust, after their shift on 17 February 1739.

He stood on a small hill and pitched his voice about one hundred metres away calling out, 'Blessed are the poor in spirit, for theirs is the kingdom of Heaven.' The miners came closer and listened as he told them a story which made them laugh. None had ever heard a preacher tell a joke; most had never heard a preacher at all. About two hundred men gathered as he spoke of hell as being as black as their pit and of the certainty of judgment. He talked about Jesus who was a friend of tax collectors and sinners, who came not to call the righteous but sinners to repentance.[5]

Eventually he began to see remarkable things. He noticed tears falling from the eyes of a young man on his right, forming a pale streak down his grimy face. He saw the same thing happen to an old bent miner on his left, and then to more and more of them. He wrote that

4.   Wesley, John, *Journal*, entry dated Saturday 31 March, 1739

5.   http://menwhosawrevival.blogspot.com/p/george-whitefield.html *Accessed 24 August 2023.*

he saw, 'white gutters made by their tears... down their black cheeks'[6] and went on, 'Blessed be God! I have now broken the ice! I believe I was never more acceptable to my Master than when I was standing to teach those hearers in the open fields.'[7]

Whitefield went on to preach outdoors to enormous crowds in both the UK and America. He once wrote: 'I now preach to ten times more people than I should, if I had been confined to the churches.'[8] He preached wherever people gathered, including at public hangings, racecourses, and carnivals, receiving plenty of abuse in the process, including having dead dogs and rotten food thrown at him.

Eventually the church authorities began to refuse the revival leaders access to their pulpits with their evangelical doctrines and unorthodox ways. On one occasion when John Wesley was forbidden to preach inside the church in his hometown of Epworth, he used his father's tombstone in the churchyard as a pulpit.[9]

All this reminds us that when God's Spirit is at work in the hearts of His people, kindling in them a deep longing for the salvation of the lost, no man-made barrier will stop them finding ways to enable as many as possible to hear the gospel. It caused Charles Spurgeon to conclude that 'it would be very easy to prove that revivals of religion have usually been accompanied, if not caused by, a considerable amount of preaching out of doors or in unusual places'.[10]

6. Gillies, John, *Memoirs of the Life of the Reverend George Whitefield,* MA (London, 1772), quoted in Dallimore, Arnold, *George Whitefield,* Volume 1, (Banner of Truth, 1970), p. 263

7. ibid., p. 256

8. Whitefield, George, *Journals* (Banner of Truth, 1986), p. 233

9. Wesley, John, *Journal,* vol. 1 (Baker, 1979), p. 377

10. Spurgeon, Charles, *Lectures to my Students* (various editions), p. 236

Incidentally, one such unusual place was employed by the seventeenth-century Church of Scotland minister John Welsh (great grandson of the Reformer John Knox) who preached in the middle of the River Tweed, which at the time marked the border between England and Scotland. Because he was banned from preaching in both countries he chose to do so when the river was frozen over, 'that either he might shun the offence of both nations, or that two kingdoms might dispute his crime'.[11] I wonder whether he feared the ice would crack under his feet as he preached and that a torrent of floodwater would sweep him away? Surely we face much less jeopardy standing to speak up in our local shopping malls!

What about some of the advantages of open-air preaching?

We've thought about the theological and historical roots of street preaching. What about the practical benefits? Does it add anything to our preaching in our church buildings and conversations with our colleagues, friends, and families?

Let me suggest a few pragmatic reasons for doing it:

Reaching the unreached

Street or open-air preaching has the benefit of being able to speak to people who may be part of the 50 per cent of the UK population who do not know a Christian, or have any idea about Christianity, and the 98 per cent who never attend an evangelical church. They get to hear *something*. It might just be a fragment as they walk by, but if done well it might be a piece of biblical truth that could have a lasting impact.

---

11.   Scott, Hew, *Fasti ecclesiae scoticanae; the succession of ministers in the Church of Scotland from the reformation*, vol. 2. (Oliver & Boyd, 1917), pp. 287-88

It also has the benefit of filtering out those who are not interested; it doesn't impose on them because staying to listen is entirely voluntary, which means that those who do stop to listen are probably interested to some degree. Someone I know preaches in shopping streets in Derbyshire where many college and university students hang out at lunchtimes. He says that most of those there will have no experience or knowledge of church or the gospel, but some of them stop, listen, and engage.

Another preacher from the West Midlands remembers being accosted by a gruff young man in a Burger King saying, 'You're that bloke that preaches aren't you?' 'I try to', he replied gently. 'Yeah, I've heard you loads of times', he said, and then went on to ask, 'Is there any hope for me?' As he then shared his testimony of deliverance from drugs and alcohol dependence and his experience of forgiveness and salvation in Jesus, the man replied, 'That's the best news I've heard all day. I've just been told I've six months to live.'

Also, think about the many who live in our towns from other countries and cultures and who follow other religions. The likelihood of them coming into a church is small and yet they might be curious. They may listen discreetly but with real interest.

An open-air preacher from London recalls a man approaching the board he was using to explain a gospel story and saying 'I am a tourist from Saudi Arabia; what is this?' The preacher was able to explain the message to him and give him a *Gospel of John* to take home.

Another man told me about a long conversation with two British Pakistani Muslims in a major UK town. They stopped to listen to the preacher and raised the usual Muslim objections but, after the preaching had finished, they were willing to speak with him and his friend.

This is not a new phenomenon. There is a story that the nineteenth-century Baptist preacher C.H. Spurgeon told about a Polish Jew who started listening to an open-air preacher out of curiosity and to improve his English and ended up being converted.[12]

We want everything to be neat and orderly; street preaching isn't like that. But it does get to the 1 in 10 or the 1 in 100 who, for a whole set of reasons, would never enter a church, but would listen to someone speaking on the street. But how will they ever hear if no such preachers are ever sent (Rom. 10:15)?

Standing out in a crowd

There is something very daunting about speaking out in a public place without a gathering of interested people already in place. The very reason we don't want to do it is probably the reason why we should: We don't want to look foolish; we don't want people to think badly of us. Of course, there may have been good reasons for not preaching on *that* particular day in *that* particular place. It was raining and standing in the middle of the water feature was not a good look. But maybe the decision against going out on the street is motivated more by fear; it actually isn't a foolish idea, but we just don't want to take a risk.

Is it that we are driven more by fear than faith? I know I am at times. We don't want to suffer the 'offence of the cross' (Gal. 5:11). Let's be honest, there's really not a lot of reputational risk for the church preacher or youth and children's worker. But open-air preaching, when we as Christians stand up in public and declare our faith in Jesus Christ, is a bold statement that we are not ashamed of the gospel. We are saying that this message is very

---

12. Spurgeon, C.H., *Lectures to my Students*, p. 256

important to us – it is the truth – and we are willing to look a bit awkward to declare it to be so.

Do you ever wonder if there were days when the Old Testament prophets or New Testament apostles might have thought, 'This is a bit embarrassing'? 'No one's going to listen and even if they do, they won't respond. I know this crowd; if I were them I don't think I'd listen either.' I'm sure they had days when they thought of a hundred reasons to rationalise their staying at home. But the only reason we have their words recorded for us in Scripture is because, whatever their natural disinclinations might have been, they overcame them and called out in the street.

If maintaining our dignity is a concern, we need to remember the example of King David. He abandoned his royal robes and danced enthusiastically as the Ark of the Covenant was returned to Jerusalem. His wife despised him for this display, but he replied 'It was before the LORD... I will become even more undignified than this, and I will be humiliated in my own eyes' (2 Sam. 6:21-22).

It might be that people will not understand and will despise you but isn't that mostly what happens to Paul in the marketplace in Athens as they call him a babbling gutter sparrow? And isn't this just what they did to Jesus?

Preach it

Although relational and conversational evangelism and Bible study are a valuable part of church life, there is something special about *preaching*. It allows the development of an argument but, more importantly, it also expresses the reality that ultimately God's Word is a declaration from Him to us. His Word is not a set of suggestions that we might consider as lifestyle options, but the proclamation of an almighty King. When the New Testament describes the early Christians going out with

79

the message, it uses words that indicate the message was proclaimed – preached. In the main, two Greek words are used (*euangelizomai* and *kērussō*); the first means the declaration of good news, and the other suggests the activity of a herald issuing a proclamation. It is true that whenever we share the news about Jesus in whatever setting, including informal conversation, we are in some sense announcing good news or making a declaration, but I would suggest these words also tell us something about the *style* employed by these first preachers which was connected to public proclamation.

But what about the disadvantages?

Those were some of the practical arguments in favour of street preaching. What about those against?

Some will say that street preaching is intrusive, perhaps even offensive. It is an imposition on those who are going about their business, on the way to the cinema, the beach or, like Prince Harry (apparently), to the TK Maxx sale. It is, they will argue, a matter of basic courtesy that we should keep our preaching for church meetings, rather than bawling in the ears of passers-by. We thus create the impression that Christians are rude, belligerent, and arrogant.

This certainly raises questions about methodology. Can we do street preaching and any follow-up dialogue in a way that isn't unpleasant or intimidating?

Others will argue that however appropriate it may appear in theory, in practice open-air preaching is simply ineffective. More people will be turned off by a street preacher than will be converted, and the statistics, they say, bear this out; in our culture it just doesn't work. People do not stop what they are doing to gather around someone speaking in the open air; they are far more likely to hurry on in embarrassment or disgust.

But is that really true? It seems to work for street entertainers. And politicians are able to draw a crowd, albeit they will bring along their own supporters to form an initial group to which passers-by can join more easily.

It could also be argued that because we are now in a post-Christian Western world, people will not understand concepts like God, commandments, sin, eternal life, or the historicity of Jesus; they simply don't have the basic biblical background to make sense of the soundbites of a street presentation.

But again, isn't this more about methodology? We already modify our preaching style and content to suit our hearers – a pre-school group will be addressed very differently to senior citizens. We do it for cross-cultural mission as well. So why wouldn't we do that on the streets in the post-Christian West?

How to do it

Having discussed the principles, we close out this chapter with a few practical considerations. This is a very simple set of reflections, as there are plenty of books and online resources which develop them in more detail and say it better than I can.

Prerequisites

Do be prayerful. I cannot believe how stupidly lacking in prayer I am many times. I know in my heart that prayer is essential but often am spiritually lazy. Pray for all the logistics; pray for the right words, pray for a hearing; pray for fruit. Most of all, pray that Christ would be honoured as He is proclaimed and that you would rejoice in this opportunity to serve Him.

Approach the whole event with enthusiasm and hope, not as something you just want to get done with and tick the box.

Work in partnership. As an absolute rule, if you want to preach on the streets make sure that you are sent by your local church and that you are accountable to its leaders. Lone rangers in any church ministry are not helpful but especially in this most public of roles. In conjunction with your church, make sure the practical issues of insurance, risk assessments etc. have been considered. This is not showing a lack of faith but a wisdom to know the realities of working in our modern world with the various legal hazards.

Practicalities

At the simplest level we should go fishing where the fish are.[13] Choose somewhere that has a reasonable footfall but at the same time make sure you are not obstructing the highway, or disrupting shoppers and traders. Parks, beaches, shopping centres, and other public spaces might be subject to local by-laws, while some may be in private ownership.

Be aware of your rights. In this area avoid the extremes of being too deferential to over-reaching authority on the one hand and actively seeking 'persecution' on the other. As Jeremy Walker helpfully writes: 'Bear in mind that arrest is not the ultimate badge of honour for the open-air preacher, some unassailable confirmation of spiritual faithfulness, the ministerial equivalent of the Victoria Cross. Sadly, some preachers seem to think that there is some scale of awards in which the more they are abused or restricted, the more effective and faithful they have been.'[14]

What will arrest people's attention? You probably have only a few seconds to convince people you have something of interest to say. Throwing out questions can sometimes

---

13. Earnest, J.P., *A Handbook on Open-Air Evangelism*, (DayOne, 2022) p. 16

14. https://www.reformation21.org/blogs/thoughts-on-street-preaching. php. Accessed 12 December 2023.

be a way of stopping passers-by. Make sure your tone is attractive; it is easy, in your nervousness and zeal, to sound angry, hostile, and unnatural. Some people use display boards to draw the eye but other objects of interest can be useful as visual aids. Do something notable. Tell a joke like George Whitefield.

Think about giveaways: books, tracts, flyers signposting church events, and other resources. Make sure they are good quality and will not be readily discarded.

Style and content

Make sure you sound as you want to be – sincere and kind. It sounds obvious, but make what you say interesting! Your speaking tone is probably the thing to reflect on the most carefully. As J. P. Earnest says, 'some street preachers... come over as quite hostile. The tone of our voice is of great importance'.[15]

Speak in short and simple sentences that are likely to be understood immediately. Don't make the reasonable assumptions that you make for regular preaching to the church – your audience is very different. Try and make connections with what people are doing, with popular culture, how they might be thinking; address the big questions of life.

Also bear in mind that there are other ways of engaging with people on the street as a 'wrap-around' to the talking part which could include:

- singing (but only if it can be done well)

- drama – acting out Bible events or parables, or some other story that will attract attention

- interviewing members of the public about an interesting question

---

15. Earnest, *A Handbook on Open-Air Evangelism*, p. 26

- dramatic readings – for example, get someone to read extracts from a Gospel. You could even read from the King James Version to give it some kind of Shakespearean feel!

At the end of your short message, make yourself available for questions and comments.

Risks

To give a complete picture, we have to talk about the dangers involved with street preaching. We have talked about the risk of feeling a bit of an idiot but there are other risks you might have to consider:

You might be abused verbally or physically

I spoke with a man who preaches regularly in a major city in the south-west of England. Once some followers of another religion bought potatoes and started throwing them at him and his team as he was speaking. His wife was hit in the chest and fell to the ground in pain. She wasn't seriously hurt, and through her tears she called her husband to keep preaching. The area fell quiet and a group of about a hundred carried on listening in rapt silence for about half an hour. That was a good outcome in many ways, but doesn't minimise the real danger of some kind of physical assault that might follow a presentation. So we need to be prepared for this. As Paul says: 'For Christ's sake, I delight in weaknesses, in insults, in hardships, in persecutions, in difficulties. For when I am weak, then I am strong.' (2 Cor. 12:10)

Having said that, we also need to be careful that we do not invite insults by conducting ourselves in an aggressive or inflammatory way that goes beyond the inevitable 'offence of the gospel'.

You might be arrested

In the UK over the last decade or so street preachers have got into trouble with the police and some have been arrested. In principle, we have a legal right to share the gospel on the streets, to read or quote the Bible and to engage in discussion, as long as we do not cause a riot, incite hatred, cause an obstruction, trespass, make too much noise, breach the peace, or commit a hate crime.[16] The law recognises five types of hate crime on the basis of race, religion, disability, sexual orientation, and transgender identity. Anyone can be prosecuted if they have demonstrated hostility, or been motivated by hostility, based on any one of these characteristics.[17]

Clearly, the judgment as to whether we have demonstrated hostility or were motivated by hostility is entirely subjective and has given rise to street preachers being arrested without proper grounds. In May 2023 Colin Bloom, the UK government's Independent Faith Adviser, published a review of 'how government engages with faith'.[18] Amongst many useful suggestions the report included the appalling idea that to call someone an apostate, unbeliever, or heretic is 'a violation of human rights' and could lead to the speaker being labelled an extremist. On this basis, most major Christian theologians and all faithful church pastors of the last 2,000 years would be deemed extremists![19]

Only God knows how this might shape new legislation in the coming years and what the consequences for open sharing of the gospel will be.

---

16. Speak Up, *Evangelical Alliance*, p. 14

17. https://www.cps.gov.uk/crime-info/hate-crime *Accessed 11 May 2023.*

18. https://assets.publishing.service.gov.uk/government/uploads/system/uploads/attachment_data/file/1152684/The_Bloom_Review.pdf

19. https://christianconcern.com/comment/bloom-review-labels-christian-words-and-practices-as-extremist/ Accessed 12 December 2023.

It might reflect badly on your church

Finally, a further risk is that any missteps on your part – or any negative response to your perfectly legal and measured sharing of the gospel – might lead to your church (and the wider church of Christ) coming to prominence in ways that might not be especially helpful. The local press might investigate and the headlines they create might make for a sensational story and a tough few weeks until the news machine has rolled on. At such times we keep praying and hold our nerve.

Street talking

Going door-to-door

My first experience of door-to-door evangelism was when I was in my twenties. I knocked at the house of someone in the street where we lived and gave her my speech and waited for her response; she said she wasn't interested. My brief planning session had been all about respecting people's space and decision not to engage, which I thought I was doing as I replied 'please yourself'. I meant it as a respectful acceptance of her desire to close the door. She heard it as a rather rude way of saying I do not agree with or care about what you think. She replied in kind as she slammed the door: 'I will please myself young man.' Here ended my door-to-door career until many years later!

In order to meet the 50 per cent of our population who are totally unreached with the gospel, we might need to get up from the sofa and bang on some doors. Al Baker, a Presbyterian pastor in America suggests that 'every church, every pastor ought to have a plan to visit regularly and systematically every household within a two-to-three-mile radius of the church building'. He suggests that we say something like this:

"'We are seeking to get to know more people in our community and we would like to invite you to our church next Sunday. May I give you some information about our church? We hope you will visit us soon. By the way, is there anything we can pray for you about today?" If the person says yes, then write down the request and offer to pray a very short prayer at their door. If no one is home, then leave a flyer about your church at the front door, and keep moving.'[20]

This is not just a good idea for pastors. This is something all of us can do. Why don't we do that?

The famous nineteenth-century Scottish church leader Thomas Chalmers was known for his promotion of works of mercy in Edinburgh alongside his other accomplishments. Chalmers was grieved that 'the vast bulk of the working population had been allowed to sink into a profound abyss of ignorance and irreligion' and 'yearned to see the organized religious resources of every branch of the Christian Church united in a coordinated attack on heathenism, destitution and ignorance.' He divided the notorious West Port slums of the city into twenty districts, of about twenty families each. A visitor was appointed to visit once a week all the families in their district. They were instructed to win goodwill by distributing tracts, entering into conversation, praying, and promoting spiritual welfare. Washrooms, a day school, evening classes, and a Sunday school were established. After about six years there was a church with four hundred members, and the school had 470 pupils attending.[21] This was house-to-house visiting on a scale that no church I know of does, but it makes you wonder, what if we did something like that?

---

20. https://banneroftruth.org/us/resources/articles/2017/case-door-door-evangelism/ Accessed 12 December 2023.

21. https://www.christianstudylibrary.org/article/door-door-visiting. Accessed 12 December 2023.

Street conversations

A variation on intruding on someone's home life by door knocking is to have 'street conversations'. There are many different ways to do this, but it essentially means to walk around public places and politely but intentionally try to engage people in conversation with questions about their faith and with an invitation to your church and the offer of prayer.

Will you go out on the street?

I started writing this chapter feeling sceptical and cautious about street preaching, but I end it feeling convicted. We should do it more! As someone who is too vain for their own good and does not relish this kind of ministry, the sacrifice required to go out on the streets is a hard ask. I would rather speak boldly to tens of thousands of people on the radio than suffer the excruciating awkwardness of speaking in the open air, but I do think street preaching and initiating one-to one conversations by visiting houses and talking to people on the street has its place alongside other forms of evangelism. I cannot ignore the biblical and historical examples.

Whatever the pros and cons, we must be realistic that this is not for everyone, but as Charles Spurgeon testified:

'No sort of defence is needed for preaching out of doors, but it would need very potent arguments to prove that a man had done his duty who has never preached beyond the walls of his meeting-house.'[22] He has a point doesn't he? Find the potent arguments against doing it; maybe ours are rather flimsy.

I think we need to be sensitive to the weather, the culture, and the law but I am left with the strong impression we could be out on the streets much more.

---

22.   Spurgeon, *Lectures to my Students*, p. 254

Even if you end this chapter still convinced street evangelism of any kind is not for you, I trust you will at least see the principles of crying aloud in your streets as the prophets of the Old Testament did, as Jesus and the apostles did, and that you will pray for and support those who do hit the streets to tell the gospel in the marketplace.

Questions for reflection and discussion

1. How do you react to the idea that street evangelism seems to have a biblical pedigree?

2. What do you like about street preaching, and what makes you feel uncomfortable with it?

3. How could you organise something in your town for door-to-door visiting or street evangelism? What holds you back from doing this?

Chapter 4

The Media Marketplace

*'Write down the revelation
and make it plain on tablets
so that a herald may run with it.'*
(Habakkuk 2:2)

In this chapter I want to talk about getting involved in the media. Most of it will be about the news media but I will also touch on the creative arts.

You might be thinking about skipping this chapter because the subject is not for you. (To be fair, you might have thought about skipping most of the other chapters for the same reason.) But think again! Let me encourage you to keep reading. I will explain why:

- you can probably be more involved than you think – read on for some ideas

- there is so much more than the national main-stream media

- it is important to be aware so you can pray for more people to be in positions of influence in the media.

What do we mean by 'the media'?

'The media' is the main form of mass communication (broadcasting, publishing etc.). It includes social media

(Facebook, Twitter etc.) and the Internet more generally. It has lots of components like print media, publishing, the news media, photography, cinema, broadcasting, streaming, podcasting, and advertising – and an overlap with the entertainment sector. But the element in common is the communication with lots of people who are not part of one individual community. Mass media thus presents to a (usually) large audience, the members of which have no explicit connection with each other except for their shared consumption of that particular information.

People sometimes differentiate between the mainstream media – referring to the traditional, long-established news outlets, owned by states or large conglomerates – and what you might call the independent media, which are smaller, non-commercial organisations.

I am going to focus in this chapter mainly on what we might call traditional media – news channels, newspapers, and radio stations – and then also think a little about using entertainment and the arts.

The state of mainstream media

The mainstream media is now a complex array of terrestrial, satellite, and streaming services which provide news, information, and entertainment programming. When I was growing up in the UK there were first three and eventually four TV channels (BBC 1, BBC 2, ITV, and Channel 4) with very specific times of day for reporting the news, for example at 1.00pm, 6.00pm, and 10.00pm. It was read seriously with a few packages of pre-recorded reports.

Radio was a bit more exciting with the BBC, the state broadcaster, dominating the airwaves along with various independent music stations that popped up, some of which became very successful. Then came satellite channels (especially Sky TV) and more radio stations, and finally with the advent of the Internet, it became possible to broadcast anything from pretty much anywhere to anyone wherever they were.

All the main TV channels have news options and there are dedicated news channels such as Sky News. Other recent entrants into the news market include GB News and Times TV. There are a plethora of radio stations, some still broadcasting via radio waves, some also on the Internet, and some just online. News and current affairs stations such as LBC and TalkRadio pretty much broadcast a 24-hour rolling output. Other stations have a mixture of news and music, while others are predominantly music stations.

There are some Christian-based broadcasters, which have a broad range of Christians and non-Christians amongst their audiences. The main Christian broadcasters include Premier Christian Radio, TWR-UK and UCB (mainly audio with YouTube clips) and new online-only entrants like Konnect Radio (who play a mixture of Christian and secular music). Christian TV stations include TBN, Revelation TV, and God TV.

Newspapers in printed form still exist of course (although does anyone wrap chips in them any more?), and these can be national, regional, or local and they all have online options. None of the national newspapers have the numbers of readers of their print versions as they had decades ago, but most have a fairly consistent and significant readership when online versions are also taken into account. For example, the *Daily Mail* has 680,000 print readers plus 150,000 online subscribers, whereas twenty years ago it was two million or more for its print-only publication.

Most of the newspapers have political sympathies which may or may not be understood by their readers, and even if understood they may not be of concern to the readers who enjoy having their biases confirmed. For those it is a bit like a clock that is always set fast – we know it is wrong but we allow ourselves to be slightly deceived by it because it helps us get to places on time.

In reporting the news, it used to be claimed by the TV channels that they were completely neutral. In reality, however, most channels, including the BBC, have some degree of bias in terms of the prominence they will give to certain stories, what questions they ask and what facts they present. This is probably a controversial view but I would suggest that this became much more obvious during the Brexit and Covid debates in the UK. To my mind there was bias, not in distortion of the facts but in the weighing of competing opinions.

Most of the media has a socially liberal bias. This becomes obvious when matters such as Christian beliefs are being discussed. Christian beliefs on creation are viewed as mythical nonsense, and so-called fundamentalist views on the exclusive claims of Christ, or about Christian ethics, are considered to be immoral and perhaps even unbroadcastable.

In the US there are even more TV channels because of the long history of cable channels way before the Internet arrived. Broadly speaking, their news channels are more sympathetic to a Christian viewpoint, but their stations are much more overtly politically aligned than in the UK.

What about being a practitioner?

Before thinking about how you might offer good news to the media locally and nationally, it is worth asking whether you, or someone in your church, would like to take up a career in the media. You could become a journalist, presenter, reporter, or producer. Journalists gather and present news and information. They should be telling you the 'who, what, where, when, and why' as truthfully and accurately as possible.

Ever since the first person ran into a crowd with news of a battle won, there have been journalists. There have been news-tellers and sometimes, even in the Old Testament, propaganda purveyors.[1] The runners coming with news of battles to the kings of Israel were journalists. The gospel writers were compilers and editors of journalistic pieces of writing. The apostles and evangelists who followed them were journalistic practitioners, faithfully telling the news about Jesus Christ with background, context, and some reporting of reaction.

Some people say journalism is right up there as a prophetic role, speaking truth to power. I am not sure about that, but we can say that genuine journalism, unravelling the truth of a story, is a noble task. Because of their commitment to truth telling, Christians should be ideal candidates for journalism, either as a reporter or somewhere in the production process.

The main caution I would offer, however, is that these days journalism is as much about entertainment through the drama, gossip, and conflicts of current affairs, as the meticulous reporting of facts. In the marketplace of media channels vying for attention, everything has to be dramatic and sensational in order to compete. A Christian will want to tell stories in an engaging way and convey the drama where there is drama but would not want to descend into the gutter.

Why be a contributor?

I also want to encourage some of you reading this book to figure out ways to get 'content' into the mass media.

---

1. Think about Sennacherib in 2 Kings 18.

This might be national but could mean local; it could be anything from interviews on primetime TV to a paragraph and a photo for a regional news website. Before we talk about what you might be able to do, I want to give you some reasons why speaking up from a Christian standpoint on a range of issues has great value.[2]

Fulfilling the Great Commission

Speaking to the crowd is part of our being faithful to the Great Commission of Jesus (Matt. 28). It is one way to follow Paul's example and speak up in the marketplace, the public square. Being evangelistic, being prophetic, genuinely speaking truth both to the powerful and the weak is a way to make and teach disciples. As they hear you, people might become interested, get saved, or at least be more sympathetic to the next Christian they meet.

I was recently interviewed about assisted suicide on a national broadcaster and BBC regional radio stations. We went through the standard arguments about whether it is more compassionate to let someone choose to die and then, out of the blue, I was asked about the hope Christians might have as they suffer. So I was able to talk about our broken world, and the hope we have by trusting Jesus. I also had a conversation with the producer on a show just moments before we were going live, who said she had recently become interested in Christianity and I was able to offer help and suggest churches local to her.

Think about the numbers of people involved. Some local networks or newspapers might have thousands of listeners/readers, BBC local radio reaches tens of thousands of people, and a national TV station might get a million or more viewers. These are huge numbers of

---

2. I am grateful to the Media Group within Affinity for their help developing this list.

people we would otherwise never be able to speak with. It is part of what it means for us to 'go to the nations'.

Encouraging Christians

Speaking up boldly encourages other Christians who are listening in that they could do something similar, maybe in the media but maybe with their friend at the coffee shop or football match. When we hear Christian truth spoken openly in a context that we were not expecting, it encourages us to realise it can be done. It gives confidence that Christians actually do have something to say in our culture and a forum in which to say it – it breaks down the barrier between what we fear cannot be done and what in fact is possible.

It also provides a model for conversations others might have. How do you graciously answer questions on Christian ethics, slavery, or gay marriage? How do you talk about Jesus, when you might not be asked directly about Him? Listening to someone else do these very things in a faithful and winsome way in the media can be a learning experience for us all.

Testing our faith

Contributing to the media helps to put our faith to the test; in the full glare of public gaze, we find that it will stand up to scrutiny. I remember being on a late-night TalkRadio show and just mentioning that there are arguments for the existence of God and the presenter being genuinely surprised and saying, 'Oh really, what are they?' And I gave some. Priceless!

Because our faith is the truth, it should be open to question. When it is, we will find it to be robust under interrogation. Think how many great speeches and sermons in the Bible would not have happened if the speaker had waited until there was a carefully organised group seated and eager to listen. Whether it was the king's court or before a riotous rabble, it was a hostile audience that in God's providence provided us with such memorable and powerful witness statements.

As well as proving our faith under public scrutiny, the media also tests us and helps sharpen up our arguments. As I have mentioned already, I used to spend time witnessing to Muslims in a UK town with a large Islamic population. I always came away from those conversations feeling pretty wretched because my answers were rather inadequate and unconvincing. It challenged me to think about the arguments I was using. I remember one time being asked, 'Where is the Holy Spirit?' My debater proceeded to jab his pointed finger at various areas of my body saying, 'Is it here?' and then saying, 'If I chopped off one of your arms would the Holy Spirit still be in the arm?' How do you answer that?

So my experience of any evangelism, and also in answering questions in the media, is that it's an excellent way to test out our arguments, to refine them and to jettison those that are not fit for purpose. Of course, we are not going to persuade anyone by our words alone. And yet God uses our words. It's better to have good arguments than weak and illogical ones.

Being salt and light

Public advocacy – speaking up on behalf of people in need and seeking to improve the lives of others by using the media – can be part of our witness. We can speak on issues relating to law and public policy. We might raise the needs of refugees, the mistreatment of a person silently praying near an abortion clinic, the plight of persecuted Christians across the world, or for minorities in our own country experiencing discrimination. In this way, our contributions can help to inform and reshape public sentiment and political opinion. Christians have a prophetic role to speak into our culture with biblical truth. If we remain silent, how will God's voice be heard?

As well as speaking out on behalf of general injustice and sin, it is also sometimes necessary to contend for our own democratic freedoms to be able to hold and promote our Christian beliefs. We do not presume that we will always be protected in law but for the moment, in the Western world, we still enjoy a large (if diminishing) measure of legal freedom of belief and expression, despite regular attempts by some authorities and activists to silence us.

If our freedom of speech continues to be eroded this will not only be bad for the church, but ultimately it will be damaging for society as a whole. If people refuse to hear the wisdom of God and His gracious appeals to turn away from our sinful folly, and reinforce that rejection by the rule of law, it is they who will suffer the most as the consequences of immorality work their way out in society.

For example, as I write, there are plans for a UK law against so-called 'Conversion Therapy'. This would make it illegal for parents, pastors, and youth leaders – anyone, in fact – to hold conversations or pray with someone in an attempt to challenge ('suppress or deny' in the words of the proposed legislation) a person's perceived sexuality or gender identity. But I am hopeful that representations and media campaigns by Christian groups and individuals will have some impact in softening some of the worst aspects of this law.

Other matters upon which we might want to speak include marriage, the family, or the right to life. There is a clear Christian position on these subjects which often fails to get a hearing. We recognise the reality that things such as abortion and gay marriage are permitted in law and encouraged in our culture, but that doesn't mean we should stop saying that they are wrong in God's eyes and bad for society.

We can, and must, speak up about all of these issues, not just to preserve freedom of expression for the sake of the church, but even more importantly for the wellbeing of society as a whole. This needs to be emphasised in our communications so that it does not appear that we are simply seeking to benefit ourselves. If God's Word is silenced by law, what hope is there for our sad and needy nation?

A trickier aspect of speaking up relates to matters upon which there is no one accepted Christian position. It could be about an issue where the principles are clear enough, but believers might be divided on how to apply them in the real world. For example, about halfway through the Covid pandemic someone complained that in my public interviews and media opportunities I hadn't commented on the reduction in Universal Credit that the government had just enacted. My answer was that I was not qualified enough to understand the issue, but with the little knowledge I did have I was not persuaded it was wrong. But even if I was convinced it was wrong, this would be a topic where I would acknowledge Christians might differ, and thus talk more about the general biblical principles of compassion, care for the vulnerable, and fairness.

Another important purpose in our media engagement is to correct all manner of widespread misunderstandings about what Christians believe and do. Biblical literacy is at an all-time low in the UK and this also affects government ministers, MPs, and civil servants who often make false assumptions about what Christianity is and how it is practised. This was seen very clearly in the many discussions that took place during Covid lockdowns between church leaders and government officials as to what constitutes a Christian worship service. So, as and when we are able, it is useful to remove misconceptions about what we actually believe about the cross, or what happens at a baptism service, or what we think about the Bible, amongst many other issues.

We can also talk about the goodness of God's commands and Christian ethics. For example, we might argue that children fare better in loving, committed, stable marriages, or that the claims of the trans rights movement are illogical, untruthful, and prejudicial against women. As a caution though, we need to make sure we are ultimately pointing people to the authority of God and His Word, not just making utilitarian arguments about what works best.

How to get into the media

In 2016, I began a new role with Affinity, a national church network organisation and one of my objectives was to speak up for conservative evangelical Christians in the public square, by which I meant the media. I had no idea how to do it. Apart from something on local radio many years ago promoting a church event, I did not have any media experience, contacts, or credibility. I had received no media training and was pretty much unknown even to Christian radio and TV news, let alone in the secular world.

In God's goodness, however, someone called me up completely out of the blue and offered his services to help get us some media interviews. This person was not from our church constituency, and to be honest I was pretty sceptical at first, but decided to give it a go and see what happens because it seemed like God was in it. Praise Him, it was a good decision!

I remember my first ever interview on radio. It was with a Christian radio station, so the questioning was pretty tame, but it was live and it was all new to me. I was in a noisy café with my new media consultant and he said, 'Do you want to do an interview now?' I said, 'What, right now? No rehearsal?' Nervously I agreed to give it a try. Almost immediately the call came on my mobile and I was live on air! I thought my responses were terrible, but apparently my piece was good enough because gradually the number of interviews grew, and in addition to the Christian stations I started getting some interviews on secular local and national radio stations.

Why the personal history? It is simply to say you don't have to be highly qualified and gifted to do this kind of thing, because I most certainly was not. People often say to me, 'I could never do what you do' and my reply is always, 'You probably could.'

I am not against media training, and I am sure I could improve greatly the clarity and presentation of what I do, but many people give interviews without any training whatsoever and they do a great job of it. So why not you? Think of a witness to an incident who is then put in front of a camera on live TV. Some panic, but the vast majority answer the questions and communicate clearly what they saw. So could you.

Most of you reading this will have witnessed to your friends in a group situation or led an evangelistic Bible study, or maybe even done some street preaching, or, as in my case, worked on building sites and been shouted at by burly contractors. If this is you, you really can handle five minutes with a radio interviewer on your favourite topic – your faith and the gospel. In almost all cases the interviewer will know less than you about the subject and you will have already heard many of their objections or counterpoints.

It's not for everyone. Some people cannot think quickly enough or become easily flustered or angry. But more of you can do it than you think. And in these days of multiple channels and news websites and the need for 24/7 content, there are so many more opportunities. Not every interview has to be a massive culture war confrontation.

News and opinion

Before we go on to consider specific ideas of what to contribute, it is useful to remember that for media output there is a significant division between *news* and *opinion*.

News is the reporting of the facts of an event – describing what happened, who was involved, when it happened, and giving any other information and background including who witnessed the events or had a perspective. As we have already noted, there are journalistic decisions on which all the possible facts are reported, and bias may influence the how interviews are introduced and the kind of questions that are asked.

Don't confuse news with information. Information is data that can be about anything at all, whereas news is some event or happening that is up to the minute, immediate and likely to be of interest to a wide audience because it has relevance for them. For example, it is no longer 'news' that England won the World Cup in 1966; this is just information – almost ancient history in fact! If we (or is it 'they'?) won it again, well that undoubtedly would be news of interest to a large proportion of the population. People's emotional investment in the success of its sporting heroes would undoubtedly make such an event a very significant news item.

Opinion, on the other hand, is an individual's view on a subject. It may include facts and reporting, but it moves beyond this to subjective analysis, perspective, and opinion. It is an argument for one point of view against possible competing assessments. Opinion may seek to persuade by presenting the facts and associated viewpoints in a way that invites agreement and challenges alternative positions.

So, a news item might report the fact that a politician proposes a change in the 1967 Abortion Act to allow terminations up to thirty-six weeks' gestation. An opinion piece would be a comment on this report and – if provided by you – it might explain why, as a Christian, you believe this proposal is wrong. You might mention the God-given dignity and value of every human life, and the violence perpetrated upon a baby in the womb and the pain and terror it feels in those moments. You could also raise the question of where such creeping changes will end – the so-called 'slippery slope' towards society's disposal of unwanted children and adults.

As Christians and churches we can share information, news, and opinions with local media. Often the sharing of our news, especially in a local context, can lead to opportunities to share our opinions, or giving an opinion might give rise to being able to share information, for example, about events at your church.

This begs the question: Is the gospel news or opinion? By definition, of course, it is the 'Good News' even though it relates to events of long ago, because it is ever fresh, novel, and relevant. And it is also news in the sense that millions of people around the world still have not heard about the life, death and resurrection of Jesus, and how we may have forgiveness and new life by putting our trust in Him.

It is also news rather than opinion because we are communicating a message from God Himself, not the subjective views of this or that person. So when we say that God wants us to live in families where the parents are a mum and a dad committed together for life, this is not our opinion but the design and purpose of God our creator. And when we use the Bible in our conversations and maybe in media interviews, we don't begin by saying, 'Here's my opinion about what happened' or 'I like to think of God as...' No, we declare the truth as revealed to us by God in the Bible. This means that when we present things in the media we should be confident to tell it as fact, not as opinion or some sort of personalised truth that will be different for each individual.

However, we will also be very aware that in a secular media context our views will be taken as no more than our personal opinion (and usually a very unpalatable one at that). So we need to be wise in how we speak, and begin where people are at (remember the example of Paul at Athens we discussed in chapters one and two?). Paul made no apology for his forthright gospel message in Acts 17, but neither did he dive straight in and hit his hearers between the eyes with it. He considered who they were, how they thought, what their prior knowledge might or might not be, what their prejudices and assumptions were – in other words, what their worldview was – and began from there.

So with all that in mind, here are some specific ideas:

Share news of upcoming events

You don't have to be a big corporation to issue a press release; you just need to be able to type sentences.

For most of us, the simplest way to begin is to inform your local radio station or newspaper (whether an actual newspaper or a web-based publication) about some event coming up in your church. Most local news outlets are desperate for copy – it's their unique selling point. So give them something to read out or put on their website; if it is intriguing enough they might even ask you for an interview. Give it to them in a form that they don't have to edit – short, sharp, and to the point. Find out what works best for them. Ask if they need pictures and what are the dimensions they prefer. Make their life easy.

Remember the difference between news and information. The times of your regular church services are not really newsworthy; it's just information. It is useful information, of course, if someone wants to attend a meeting, but it's not news. Your church service times need to be on all your 'noticeboards', but like a train timetable it is only relevant if you actually want to travel. However, a new train service, added to the timetable – now that is news. There might be something about the time or destination that attracts new travellers. Likewise, a special service, or a new toddler group meeting on Saturday mornings can be newsworthy; it may be of interest to a range of people.

We can share news about a special meeting with a guest speaker who has an interesting story to tell or a challenging topic to discuss. That's a good idea, right? You want more people to come. People in church will invite their friends and family, but you want to cast the net wider. So go for it and get it into the media. But make sure when you write your flyer or press release that you first figure out what it is that you want to communicate. How will this read to the average person in the street? How will it sound when read out on the radio? What will it contain in terms of a 'hook' to make them consider coming?

Think about headlines and key points. Don't give more information than you need. Give focus to the 'what' and the 'why' and then point people to the 'where' and 'when'.

Share news of events that have happened already

News can also be about something that has already taken place. It could be about anything. Your church may have put on a tea for lots of local elderly people to celebrate the Coronation or Christmas. Perhaps you ran a holiday club for kids in the area and everyone had a great time, even though they were all drenched by a huge downpour! Maybe you have just calculated that your church foodbank helped more clients than ever before this year. You just opened a coffee shop. Six people were baptised. A church member had a liver transplant and testified to how God helped her trust Him through an immensely stressful time.

Try to create a brief but interesting story of what happened; the media loves stories. Could you illustrate it with a novel picture? I recently heard an interview with a guy who dressed up as an eagle outside a fish and chip shop to scare away the seagulls. He got on prime-time BBC national radio to talk about it! Yet he was an ordinary person with no media training. You don't have to dress up as an eagle (even if some of you might enjoy it), but be inventive and do something newsworthy in order to begin to develop a media presence, especially locally, and hopefully invitations will come to write or speak again. Then over time you may find that you are able to contribute more serious, gospel content.

Don't think of this as using gimmicks or marketing to 'sell' the gospel in a dishonourable manner. The Old Testament prophets, the apostles, and even Jesus Himself used drama, humour, hyperbole, visual aids, and rhetorical devices to get our attention and to get the message across.

Give a view on everything

As your opportunities grow you may become a known and trusted voice to comment on all sorts of things. Because all of creation belongs to God, there is not a square inch of it that we cannot speak into. You might begin by commenting on general things that people talk about in their daily lives: the economy, gardening, technology, cars, politics, health, peace and security, the environment, education, and even the pandemic (as I am sure we will still be talking about it way after this book is published).

But it may be that eventually you are trusted to comment on matters that are more controversial, about which as Christians we have a distinctive and less welcome viewpoint: family, relationships, love and marriage, identity, racism, sexuality and gender, the right to life, freedom of speech, and so on.

How can you best make your views known?

- Write a short statement and send it to all the news desks and editors that you know of (if you don't know any yet, they're pretty easy to find with a simple search online).

- Share the news item you are engaging with on social media and make a brief comment.

- Write a blog about it on your church website and share this with a pithy comment inviting engagement with the piece and discussion.

- Record a short video with your opinion piece. Don't agonise over the precise words and the quality; just speak naturally and calmly, slightly slower than you would normally, but not painfully so.

Now it's worth saying that some people, especially those who have popular Christian blogs or a social media presence, seem to think their view on any and every topic is essential, and they make sure we all hear of it. This is not what I am talking about; we could do with a few less of those opinions.

You are not trying to impress your Christian friends; that is just vanity, and it doesn't build God's kingdom. But expressing a simple, humble opinion can create healthy dialogue with people who are not Christians.

Call a phone-in

The rise of 24/7 news and current affairs programming across all platforms means that editors are always on the lookout for new contributors – there are only so many journalists, experts, and politicians to be interviewed for every story. Radio, in particular, has embraced the phone-in programme format to enable members of the public to participate in discussions and debate on news items.

So why not call in with an opinion? It is best not to start with a 'repent or burn' rant, but if the context is appropriate, there should be opportunities to give a Christian perspective if you do a little preparation before going on-air.

Get an interview

If your church is particularly active in the community and you become known for this, you might attract the attention of a local or national radio or TV station when they are on the lookout for someone to interview, perhaps on a subject on which they imagine Christians might have something to say. Until you become a trusted interviewee (when they will just invite you straight into the conversation) a researcher will likely contact you for a pre-interview chat. Don't be alarmed. They are not trying to catch you out. This is their way of deciding how you will work with the news item and so they can prepare the interviewer, who will probably be reading from a script.

So, let's imagine you get your moment in the media, whether it is local or national. Here are some suggestions for the before and after:

Prepare, but don't prepare too hard

A media interview is not a lecture to read out, or a sermon, or an acting audition. So don't use a script – you will end up reading it and sounding like it. And it's actually much harder to read a script than just to talk extemporaneously. TV presenters practise a lot to read autocues well and even then it doesn't often sound natural.

However, you should make sure you know the topic you are going to talk about. Be very clear on any facts you use so you are not wrong-footed if challenged. (If that does happen just accept it, move on, and think about it later.) If it helps, have some prompts in front of you. These could be words or sentences, perhaps a key phrase that you would really like to get in the conversation:

- '...the most loving thing to do is to tell the truth...'

- '...people are hurting because they know there's something wrong...'

- '...if there is a God, surely it is OK for Him to make the rules...'

- '...the evidence for God is everywhere...'

Speak normally to the person interviewing you

In a radio or TV interview speak like you would normally do in any lively conversation. Don't come over as intense and argumentative, but neither should you be so laid-back that you leave long pauses before answering questions. My own technique is to focus on the other person and their question, not to think about the listeners or how I am sounding. I try to stay in the flow of the conversation and lean into the question with all my mind.

Tell the truth

This might seem obvious, but not surprisingly, the temptation to sugar-coat or fudge a particularly hard truth can trip you up. So, for example, if you get asked what Christians think of other religions, don't try for an over-complicated response that highlights elements of shared beliefs with other faiths. Unfortunately, the news media rarely give time for developing detailed arguments. So just say it as it is. As another example, if you're asked whether it is possible to be a 'gay Christian', you might respond by saying, 'Yes, of course, because salvation is not something I can earn by how I live. However, a Christian will want to obey God and homosexual practice is against His commands.' Incidentally, in my experience the distinction between homosexual attraction and practice is usually lost in a fast-moving interview so unless they make a point of it, it is probably better to let it go.

Answer the question – even if it is unexpected

I have often been frustrated by being asked questions I didn't want to answer which had nothing to do with the topic being considered. For example, I was once being questioned about prayers in Parliament and the interviewer switched topic to ask me, 'What would you do if your daughter told you she is gay?' Unless it is a deeply personal question that you really don't want to (and shouldn't have to) answer, give it your best shot, again trying to imagine you are chatting with a friend or one of the people on an evangelistic course. Never allow yourself to show frustration or anger, or sound patronising.

Don't be daunted by hostility – keep smiling, even on radio

Aggressive questioning is quite possible, so be ready for it. Try not to crumble on the one hand or respond in kind on the other. If your mind goes blank under fire, or you feel yourself intimidated, keep in mind the main thing you want to get across and come back to it calmly and clearly – and smile! I don't mean an inane grin that is obviously forced, but a relaxed contented smile; remember that this interview is a privilege and the person you are speaking to and the many other listeners need to know the love of Jesus.

If, on the other hand, you find yourself getting angry and wanting to come out with some sarcastic comment or put-down, consider the example of Jesus. He often faced hostile debaters, and while He at times expressed exasperation at unbelief, and could denounce in withering terms people such as the Pharisees who were wilfully blind, He was always patient and compassionate with those who were lost in their sin and confusion. Try to be the same.

Sort the technology

Make sure you know how you will be interviewed. If you are on a phone line, make sure you have a good connection. Similarly, if it is going to be a video call, make sure the signal is clear and the microphone and camera are operating well. Get yourself framed well in the picture with good lighting and with nothing distracting in the background.

In all cases when you are being interviewed at home, make sure you will not be interrupted by other phones, notification tones, doorbells, children, dogs, or anyone else in the house. It was amusing once upon a time but that era has long gone.

You are an ambassador

When you speak to the media, you are not just conveying information; your character is also being judged. You are personifying the truth of Christ; you are representing

Him. If the questioning is difficult, remember that it is not ultimately you who is on trial, but Jesus. This is a comfort, but also a challenge: Am I representing Him well? What would Christ have said? How would He have reacted?

Pray

I put this at the end not because it is the least important. On the contrary, it is vital but often gets forgotten. Pray for the right questions to come up and for you to have the right answers. Pray you would represent Christ well in the character you display and the words you use. If possible, get a group of friends together who can pray for you while the interview is taking place.

Creative media

Mass forms of communication are not limited to written and spoken words. We should also consider briefly the creative arts, especially the ones which communicate words and ideas. We cannot say for sure, but I doubt very much that the Apostle Paul engaged in street art or busked at the agora in Athens! But I do want to suggest that some art – what we might call communicative art, can be a way to provoke spiritual interest and communicate gospel ideas.

Art

We are invited as part of the mandate given us by God in creation to rule and subdue (Gen. 1:28). In doing so we should reflect the creative genius of the God who made a world of such outstanding beauty for all our senses to appreciate. We too can create items of beauty and complexity and in so doing provoke curiosity and wonder that echoes in some small way our creator and points to Him.

The Athens marketplace was a centre for the arts of its day. There were vendors of fabrics and other artefacts displaying the skill and imagination of their designers. Even more significantly, the marketplace was a location for the staging of plays, gymnastic performances,[3] and making of speeches. As I have already mentioned, the stories and plays of Greek culture were probably more influential than the famous Athenian philosophers when it came to shaping popular views about religion.

The early chapters of Genesis describe the God-given gifts that gave rise to various forms of artistic expression amongst the early humans. In Genesis 4, Jubal is described as 'the father of all who play stringed instruments and pipes' (v. 21), while his brother was a farmer, and his half-brother an engineer who 'forged all kinds of tools out of bronze and iron' (v. 22). While some people might consider making music not a particularly productive activity, certainly when compared with farming and engineering, the fact that the Bible mentions it here suggests this is a gift worthy of development and practice.

Famously, later in the Old Testament, David played music on his harp to soothe King Saul (1 Sam. 16:14-23), and it was later to play a key role in the temple worship of God (see, e.g. 1 Chron. 25). David also danced before the LORD (2 Sam. 6:14-22), which might be considered as expressive art (although not when I do it!).

We are also told in Exodus 31 that God bestowed artistic gifts upon two men, Bezalel and Oholiab, to design and make the furnishings of the desert tabernacle that would hold the Ark of the Covenant and be the focus of Israel's worship. God told Moses that He had 'filled him (Bezalel)

---

3.   https://www.britannica.com/topic/agora. Accessed 12 December 2023.

with the Spirit of God, with wisdom, with understanding, with knowledge and with all kinds of skills – to make artistic designs for work in gold, silver and bronze, to cut and set stones, to work in wood, and to engage in all kinds of crafts' (vv. 3-5).

It therefore seems a good and appropriate thing for Christians to be involved in the arts of all descriptions, expressing something of the creative mind of God Himself, and adding beauty and richness to all of life. In this way God is honoured and glorified, and such artists, if doing their work from a position of Christian faith, can be an influence for good. This is especially strategic as the creative industries are often particularly unfriendly towards God and biblical ethics.

How can Christians use their art for communicating with the lost? Not every piece of art will be seen or experienced by large crowds. It might stay in your house or be sold in a local shop for just one consumer to enjoy. But as they begin to gather an audience for their work, artists may draw attention to their faith if asked about the inspiration behind a particular piece. A gorgeous piece of pottery or sculpture might be created with the glory of God in mind. Sometimes an artist is even more explicit in their work, depicting a biblical event or engraving a Scripture text or other explanation in words on the artwork.

But some art, and especially performing arts, attract vast crowds, and some artists have millions of people who engage with their work. Art can thus be a form of mass communication. Obviously the more explicit the message in the piece is, the better able it will be at introducing people to Jesus. So in terms of reaching the unreached, I would favour word-based artistic endeavours.

Using art as a way to enhance, explain, and illustrate our message seems a perfectly reasonable thing to do.

Write something

A book, poem, or play

The Bible uses artistic methods to get the message across.

Large sections of prophetic stories of the Old Testament and the parables of the New Testament were pieces of creative art, inviting our imagination and entering into the emotion of a situation. Jesus made up stories to communicate spiritual ideas, and the apostles use analogies to illustrate their point. The last book of the Bible, Revelation, is an outstanding work of literature describing the spectacular visions of John.

Works of fiction always have some message, even if they are written for entertainment with no explicit agenda. Books and poems make us think. They communicate something about our values. Consider how contemporary culture uses kids' books and TV shows to normalise extramarital relationships or promote transgender propaganda. So could you write a book or a poem which has its own internal integrity as a piece of art, but which also gets people thinking about the gospel?

Maybe you could write a play. It might address some key cultural or social issue, and in so doing raise questions and hint at some answers. Or you might want to dramatise an event from biblical or church history, making a more explicit point along the way.

A song

Some people are gifted at writing and performing songs, combining great music with thought-provoking words. Could you write a song about how the cross impacted your life? Maybe you could write something to illustrate some aspect of theology to get people thinking. Could you write a love song with a Christian ethos? Could you compose something that critiques an aspect of the contemporary non-Christian worldview?

Questions for reflection and discussion

1. What are the advantages and disadvantages of getting involved with the media?

2. What could you and your church do to become better known by your local media?

3. The Bible is a piece of literature – factual but also containing artistic devices. Is that true and what does it say about our use of art to communicate the gospel?

Chapter 5

The Worldwide Market

'Those who had been scattered
preached the word wherever they went.'
(Acts 8:4)

Everywhere, all the time

The online world is one that constantly demands our attention. In directing your eyes to read this book you have overcome many distractions, especially the electronic ones. It's an influence which, at times can be unhelpful and addictive, but let's be honest, the Internet is a marketplace almost all of us visit and most of us spend considerable time browsing there.

What would you do if you wanted to find out the approximate number of Native Americans living in the USA today? You would search the Internet. (To save you the trouble the answer is approximately seven million – 2 per cent of the population.) Where did you go to read the news today? Where do you go when you're watching a TV show and you can't remember which movie you saw that actor in previously? Where do you buy a lot of your electronic gadgets, groceries, and garb? Where did you get this book? Where are you doing most of your reading? Where did I recently find out about the death of two prominent Christian leaders within hours of those events?

There are 5.16 billion Internet users worldwide[1] which means 64.4 per cent of the world's total population.[2] In the UK and USA over 90 per cent of the population have Internet access. Smartphones and tablets have transformed the way we interact with the Internet, giving us a sense of being always online in a way that previously unconnected PCs and laptops could not do.

The average person in the UK or the USA spends at least five hours per day on the Internet in addition to work-related access. A high proportion of this will be on entertainment (streaming services, YouTube, and gaming), but a significant time is also spent on social media and conventional websites.[3] There are over four billion active social media users, nearly 60 per cent of the world's population.[4] Over 86 per cent of the United Kingdom's total Internet user base (regardless of age) used at least one social media platform in January 2023.[5]

Sociologists tend to divide the population by age in this way:

- 'Gen Z' (born between 1997 and 2012) who will make up 27 per cent of the global working age population by 2025[6]

- 'Millennials' (born between 1981 and 1996)

---

1. In this book we use billion to denote 1,000 million (the US convention that the UK adopted in the 1970s).

2. https://datareportal.com/reports/digital-2023-global-overview-report. Accessed 12 December 2023.

3. https://www.statista.com/statistics/507378/average-daily-media-use-in-the-united-kingdom-uk/ Accessed 12 December 2023.

4. https://datareportal.com/reports/digital-2022-april-global-statshot. Accessed 12 December 2023.

5. https://www.meltwater.com/en/blog/uk-social-media-statistics. Accessed 12 December 2023.

6. https://www.theguardian.com/society/2023/jun/07/power-hungry-hedonists-survey-reveals-what-drives-generation-z. Accessed 12 December 2023.

- 'Gen X' (born between 1965 and 1981)
- 'Baby Boomers' (born between 1946 and 1964)
- 'The Silent Generation' (born between 1925 and 1945)

Nearly all of those age groups use the Internet in some way, apart from the older end of the 'Silent Generation'. The difference is in the way they use it and the proportion of time each group gives to using it for communication, information gathering, and building community. It seems clear that older generations are more selective and functional about their use of the Internet, mainly for purchasing and communicating. Years ago, my mother used to ring me up to tell me she had sent me a text message! Clearly, older users have moved on since then to become the so-called 'silver surfers', using the 'interweb thing' regularly (although not always securely). It is not their primary source of information or socialising.

The 'Baby Boomers' are a mix of the tech-savvy and tech-cautious, partly depending on their work experience, but many are established on social media and would use the web for booking tickets and watching news.

Beyond that, the later generations have grown up with more and more technology, especially 'Millennials' and even more so 'Gen-Z'. But their use tends to be social interaction and targeted news gathering (say for particular sports). Top concerns for both 'Millennials' and 'Gen-Z' are the cost of living, climate change, and mental health. The vast majority of 'Gen Z's (87 per cent) and 'Millennials' (80 per cent) use social media to consume news, influenced more by what their friends and family might be re-posting on these channels, rather than national news providers. The constant flow of information from social media and the 24-hour news cycle is a likely contributor to stress levels among those who consume it. More than six in ten

'Gen Zs' (63 per cent) and 'Millennials' (61 per cent) say they frequently or occasionally limit their exposure to news and current affairs to protect their mental health.[7] They want to be rich, powerful, and have fun but at the same time they are scared with the way the world is going.

'Gen Z' is more likely to value power, achievement, hedonism, and stimulation than other generations. Young people have always been motivated by ambition – to progress and achieve personal success as well as social standing and power. But as this has become more pronounced in the present generation their stress levels have multiplied due to a combination of economic and other challenges, alongside lives dominated by social media – the ultimate platform for demonstrating success, social standing, and aspirational lifestyles.[8]

As a real-life example, I asked some young people in my church to give me the statistics on their social media usage. In the most extreme example, for just one week, one of them reported these activity figures, as recorded by their phone:

Snapchat: 23 hours 52 minutes

TikTok: 21 hours 3 minutes

Yes, that really is in *one week*. Now, apparently, it was during the school holidays, which, maybe skews the figures slightly, but losing almost two full days on messaging and videos is quite a chunk of time. Just reflect on that. Compared to the time at church and the other input Christian parents and youth leaders might give to them, that person spent close to two whole days on social media. It's a discipleship challenge for sure.

This generation knows up-to-the-minute news about their football team but would have less interest about the

7.   https://www.deloitte.com/content/dam/assets-shared/legacy/docs/deloitte-2023-genz-millennial-survey.pdf?dl=1. Accessed 12 December 2023.

8.   https://bcwmovatory.com/bcw-age-of-values-2023-report/ Accessed 12 December 2023.

war in Ukraine. If you're a 'Baby Boomer' looking down on these guys, try checking your own usage. I glanced at mine for today and I spent six hours online. Now some of that was for writing this book which we could maybe call 'work', but social media apps were a couple of hours' worth as well. Today at least I was following some Christian threads but again it's a lot of time out of my day that I am glued to a small screen. I wonder how often you have checked your phone messages, emails, or social media since you started reading this chapter? A reasonable estimate seems to be that most people online check around 100 times per day, which is about every ten minutes during their waking hours.

Accordingly, we could spend time dwelling on the challenges of Internet use, but that's for another time and another publication. For now, I want to suggest that this scale of social media and other online activity means this is a marketplace we should definitely consider utilising for the gospel.

The agora in Athens was a place for trade, information sharing, socialising, entertainment, religion, and political debate. The Internet is an information hub, a trading floor, a space for social interaction (of sorts), politics, and religion. It is a gathering place, albeit the meetings are less visible and participants are generally less committed than those who meet in person.

Some Christians don't want to have anything to do with the Internet, apart from the barest minimum to enable them to get by; they believe it to be a source of much evil and mindless distraction. Others are equally cautious, not so much out of principle but because they don't understand it well enough, and fear that they will be scammed, or if they join an online discussion they will get millions of people 'piling on' against them.

I understand those concerns, but I do not think we can say that this technology is intrinsically bad. The purposes of organisations using it can be, and we ourselves may use it in ways that fuel lust, greed, and vanity.

But it can also be used for good. 'So whether you eat or drink or whatever you do, do it all for the glory of God' (1 Cor. 10:31). We can use the Internet in creative ways for the Lord. As we saw in chapter three, Jesus and the apostles used all possible means to reach people and I would tentatively suggest (and then run for cover) that Paul would have used email, had it been available in his day, for sending his epistles.

He might have included in that email the phrase 'everything is permissible but not everything is beneficial' (1 Cor. 10:23). We need to be aware that many of the Internet programs we use are designed to be addictive, so we will almost certainly need to put measures in place to limit our usage to wise levels so that other areas of life are not compromised. We need to encourage ourselves and our children to have a good balance of activity and to make sure we enjoy non-virtual experiences 'in the moment'.

So, we should not simply avoid it because of these dangers. Vast numbers of people who need to hear more about Jesus spend enormous amounts of time in these online spaces. This is a marketplace we need to visit as well if we want to share the gospel. So maybe we could redeem the hours we spend doom-scrolling or reel-sharing and do something evangelistic on the web.

Let me say something a bit controversial. I have sat in conferences with well-educated people, many of them middle-aged and middle-class, who criticise 'Gen Xs', 'Millennials', and 'Gen Zs' who (for different reasons for each demographic) are spending too much time on the Internet and not reading enough books and climbing trees. I feel it with them. And yet I think there is a kind of snobbery in these attitudes. Reading books really isn't for everyone. In fact, for most of the history of the church vast numbers of Christians have been illiterate and reliant on their leaders to tell them the gospel and read the Bible to them (and sadly, in some cases, not doing either).

Let's accept the dangers and the dark side, and enter this part of the market with our shields up and an egg timer set, but at least let us get into it. So where should we start? Here are some pointers. Some things we can pretty much do as individuals; some we can only do as churches or Christian organisations, and I will try and make clear the distinctions as we go along.

A website – your shop window

How do people find out about the Christian faith, especially those who do not have Christian friends or family? A large proportion go to the Internet and use a search engine. They are your market browsers. In fact, according to the 'Talking Jesus' survey, of those people trying to find out about the Christian faith, 26 per cent – the largest group – would go to a search engine rather than any other source of information.[9]

So we need to think about your church website. How are people going to find your church online? And what will they find when they get there?

You might be relieved to know that I am not going to cover lots of technical stuff about search engine optimisation, keywords, platforms, back-ends, front-ends, and plug-ins. These are the things that will help your site get noticed amongst all the other things vying for the highest rankings on search engines. If you know, you

---

9. 'Talking Jesus' report, https://talkingjesus.org/2022-research/ p. 13. Accessed 12 December 2023.

know, and if you don't you need to find someone who does! I want to focus more on the principles.

Who is your church website actually for?

Apart from a few bashful groups, in the past, churches normally announced themselves on their street with a board advertising their service times and some other key information. It might also have a Scripture verse or a pithy saying. You might therefore think that your church should basically make a digital noticeboard. That's how most started out when churches began to use the Internet. Some of them still look like it today. It is obviously useful for people to know what's happening, but I don't think this is ever that effective in attracting curious web browsers. A website can be a much richer interface than that, so why would you not make the most of it?

You also want to make yourself known to visiting Christians or those moving to your area and looking for a church to join so there are a few essential things that you might want people to know. Your own members may use the site to find out what is happening this week or when the next all-age service is.

But if you are serious about reaching out into the marketplace, you will want to keep seekers in mind when you design the site. This is your online brochure and you will want to do it well; it lets people know what to expect if they turn up on Sunday. People have turned up to our church who have found us on the website and know our leadership team quite well already, based on looking around the site and listening to or watching the sermons. In the digital-image age people do, rightly or wrongly, make some of their judgments about a church based on the quality of a website. And that is not just Christians looking for a new church. It can be non-Christians, lapsed Christians, and people of different nationalities.

You don't want to put people off with a poorly designed, uninformative website.

Let's say a couple of things about the 'boilerplate' stuff – the standard text that every site needs to include.

The welcome fallacy

Nearly all churches claim to be welcoming, friendly, and diverse. I don't think it is useful to say this. Let people decide for themselves. If you meet someone for the first time and they tell you 'I am a nice person with a great sense of humour', you would consider it presumptuous and arrogant. It is much better to say that everyone is welcome, and then (if it is true!) describe the diverse nature of your congregation – that you have young and old people and different nationalities, and that people with all kinds of backgrounds, culture, challenges, and viewpoints are part of the family.

Use photos thoughtfully

My observation is that church websites often use photographs to try to look like the biggest Christian festival, or they choose pictures which look like a tea party in a care home. Hopefully your church is somewhere in between these extremes. Why not use a couple of photos to show browsers that you are normal human beings. But don't go mad and try to recreate your family photo album – you only have a few seconds when people land on your website to get them to stay, so make them count.

Engaging with non-Christians

Bear in mind also that people don't go online simply for information but to learn new things, to get answers to questions, and to connect. So how can you use your website, and social media (which we'll talk about soon) to engage with people who are not Christians? We need to think of creative ways of using it as a tool for evangelism, outreach, engagement, and signposting.

You should think about who these people are whom you want to reach; their age, background, class, and the stage of faith (believers, lapsed, unbelievers, or agnostic). This will help you decide what content you should use and where it should go on your site to achieve your purpose most effectively. Do they need answers to big questions? If so, what questions are they asking? What is going to serve them and resonate with them the most?[10] Do you want non-Christians to attend an event? Is part of your website there so that parents will feel confident to send their kids to your clubs? Are you seeking to influence people worldwide to take an interest in the gospel? What pathways will you create to enable people to find out more or bring them to a meeting?

How are you going to do that? What will draw them in? I don't have all the answers, but maybe you can find some creative people who will come up with ideas once you have decided what you want to do.

For example, you could post a weekly sermon specifically with unbelievers in mind. You might already do this as a catch-up for the congregation who missed the service, or as a way to inform Christians looking for a church as to the type of Sunday ministry to expect. But evangelistic messages, perhaps shorter in length and with titles aimed at provoking interest in seekers, would have a more precise target audience. Or you could use just extracts of your sermons to raise a question and point to biblical answers, maybe to offer hope to the searching and the suffering.

What about producing videos answering various apologetic questions? (You can also share content like

___
10. https://fiec.org.uk/resources/your-churchs-digital-presence. Accessed 12 December 2023.

this on social media – see below.) What about telling stories? Everyone in your church has a testimony of how they came to faith, and these days it is easy to make a good quality recording of them speaking about this.

There is even a modern trend to go for 'shaky-hand, real-feel' videos, which means you could dispense with an expensive tripod-mounted camera (as long as the audio quality is still decent, which is not always a straightforward matter). Equally interesting are stories about how Christian faith makes a real difference in someone's life; it speaks to the relevance and authenticity of God's Word and power at work in our lives.

The thing to remember is that your website is like a street preacher who has perhaps just a few seconds to grab the attention of someone as they walk past – so use those moments well.

Having read all the above, you might think that your church doesn't have the resources to do any of this. My advice in that case is to keep your website very simple and use it mainly as an information board; do a few pages really well, and then maybe focus on some of the social media ideas (below) to engage outsiders.

What can you do as an individual?

As well as the church website, some of you might want to write your own individual Christian blog. You might be encouraged by your church leadership to do so as an extension of the church's own outreach. Or maybe you will do it as your own personal initiative.

If you do it yourself, and you also have your own social media accounts, there can be a degree of crossover between the two, although your blog should be the place for longer-form writing. But your posts don't have to be essays; even a few hundred words written well can have an impact.

Here are some ideas about what you could write about:

- suffering and pain, and how you deal with them as a Christian

- parenting

- a Christian approach to business

- lifestyle choices

- answering a series of questions as to why you believe or act as you do

- write about part of the Bible that you are studying and what it means to you

It's not about having some knock-out apologetic site that will intellectually dazzle, but about showing what your faith means to you, so when people stumble onto the site it draws them in.

Social media

What is social media?

Social media is a term used to describe any Internet site or application that lets you, the user, create and share information, ideas, interests, and opinions. It does this by facilitating virtual communities. They're called 'social networks' because they enable a form of social interaction among groups of people, which is different in nature to one-to one communication via email. The people who interact in this way might be well known to each other outside of the virtual group or maybe have only ever met online. They might all be living in the same town or they could be spread across the world. This sort of interaction might not be your definition of what it means to be 'social' or 'sociable', but this is how very many people interact today, as we will see.

That's a lot of sociable people

Some of what I write here will possibly be outdated by the time you read this book, such is the fast-moving nature of technological change and our interaction with it. But as a snapshot at the time of writing, here are the top ten social media platforms worldwide with some idea of the quantity[11] and demographics of their user base:[12]

1. *Facebook* is the number one with nearly three billion users worldwide. It enables the sharing of photos and provides links to videos and text. It was pretty much the first such platform to the market. The largest age group of users on Facebook is the 25–34s, but anecdotally their numbers and the amount of time spent on the site is starting to decline, and those that are still on Facebook now prioritise other social media platforms. There is an urban myth that Facebook is mainly used by middle-aged women, but that doesn't seem to match the research. It has forty-five million users in the UK, about half of which are men, some of them are even young men, despite its weakening appeal to the younger age groups. Like all the other platforms, users include many corporations and organisations – and churches.

2. *YouTube* is a hybrid of a social media platform and an entertainment and streaming site. It is second in popularity with 2.2 billion users who are pretty well represented across all the age bands.

3. *WhatsApp* is another cross-breed between a messaging service and a social media platform. It has two billion users mostly sending messages, making

11. https://www.searchenginejournal.com/social-media/biggest-social-media-sites/#close. Accessed 12 December 2023.

12. https://sproutsocial.com/insights/new-social-media-demographics/ Accessed 12 December 2023.

arrangements and sending pictures of their night out, restaurant food, or latest puppy, but it also facilitates group discussion. It's actually the number one social media platform in the UK.

4. *Instagram* is mainly a photo and short video sharing platform, but it has a growing functionality to provide links and longer videos. It also has two billion users, the vast majority of which (about 70 per cent) are under thirty-five. Instagram is a bit different from Facebook and Twitter, because its content is only visible to people within your circle of friends. It has been hugely successful with short-form videos, known as 'reels'.

5. *TikTok* is a platform designed for people to share short videos, often of themselves engaged in some form of activity and usually including music. It has about a billion users, a large proportion of whom are under twenty-five. For a simple application that in principle is not much different to other social media apps, it is a phenomenal success.

6. *Snapchat* allows users to send and receive photos and videos. Its original unique feature was the ability to send self-destructing photos and messages. It has around 500 million users.

7. *Pinterest* was an application I had almost forgotten about. They have 444 million active users, mostly under thirty-five and predominantly female. It is usually used to find recipes and find style or product recommendations.

8. *Reddit* is more of a forum-style social news website where content is socially curated and promoted by site members through voting. The content is

often suitable for adults only. It has 430 million users worldwide.

9. *LinkedIn* is a professional networking application with 250 million users. It started as a platform to link people with other people they had worked with and for, to make new connections to help your business. In practice these days it functions in a similar way to Facebook, but more for people who want to promote something to help them in their work.

10. *X* (formerly known as Twitter) is a micro-blogging short message, photo, and video posting application which has 217 million users across the world. Its usage is proportionately greater in the UK with at least twenty million users, making it the number five application for this country, and ranking similarly in the USA.

How can we witness on social media?

Apparently (in the USA at least), about a third of Christians share their faith via social media through posts, comments, and profiles; many Christians believe that technology and digital interactions have made evangelism easier.[13] What exactly they are sharing I am not so sure about. The young people I speak to in the UK are extremely wary of sharing anything about their faith on social media in case they get push back.

How could social media be good for evangelism?

• Social media extends our reach; most of us have a greater set of digital contacts than we would regularly be able to speak to. And should those conversations be shared even more widely, the overall audience could be vast.

13. https://www.barna.com/research/evangelism-in-a-digital-age-an-infographic/ Accessed 12 December 2023.

- It is not so personally challenging as when speaking face to face with someone. Our 'listeners' can choose whether to engage or not.

- It allows us some space when questions come back to take as much time as we need to reflect and answer carefully (or not in some cases!).

However, this form of interaction for evangelism and apologetics also has its downsides:

- Misunderstandings can easily happen, and they are harder to detect when dealing remotely with others. Unresolved, this may then rapidly develop into an argument or the breaking of the online relationship.

- There is no easy way to put our comments in context and to convey the right tone and intensity – emojis are not enough.

- Social media conversations are very fragmented. They can develop over minutes or months and they have no end point. They can be good and lively but then suddenly everyone moves on to do something else and the window of opportunity is lost as our device windows fill up with the latest new posts (on other subjects) by our friends. This makes the development of a careful explanation of the gospel very difficult.

- Social media allows us to form carefully curated versions of our lives which don't match our character. The temptation to be inauthentic is very real.

There is also the danger that we use social media posting and chatting as a substitute for the more difficult – and often more pressing and appropriate – witness to family and friends. The latter requires more courage on our part and more time and sacrifice to develop these friendships.

Despite all these potential drawbacks, on balance I would still highly recommend utilising social media for evangelistic purposes, as long as we do not do so to the detriment of our personal and church relationships and witness. This being so, the greatest asset you have is your set of social media friends. Most non-Christians are more likely to respond positively to a post by someone they know, or have built some online trust with, than a random church or stranger.

There are many excellent online evangelistic video shorts, graphics, and clips that are easy to share. If your own church has produced such content, do make sure you share it. It is amazing to me how many church members just look at the good content that churches and Christians produce, and don't 'like', 're-post' or 'share' it.

Remember when assessing what is genuinely worth passing on to your social media contacts, that we constantly face the temptation to reshape our message to pander to people's perceived needs and desires. This distorting of the truth may come in the guise of wonderfully entertaining and attractive media posts, but that must never take precedence over the actual truth of the message conveyed. What is the value of hundreds or even thousands of views of your post if it presents a distorted gospel?

In any case, what we have in Christ is far better and worth declaring as best we can. The gospel speaks to the real, deepest needs of the human heart and has the power to transform even the most hedonistic person, with true pleasure that only comes from a relationship with Christ. We will not sugar-coat the message or downplay the suffering that He calls His followers to embrace, but we know our restless search for identity is fully satisfied in Him.

What to post?

As churches

You need to think about what you are trying to achieve with these posts, but whatever it is, make your content interesting!

As already mentioned, you might consider using sermon extracts that carry an evangelistic punch, or short testimony videos that provoke thought or provide answers to questions non-Christians may be asking. Point to a blog that they might find interesting. Advertise an upcoming gospel event at your church by all means, but realise this: the reach of such information will be severely limited unless it is widely shared. If it is only seen by your own followers, who are probably all Christians, what's the point? However, if they all share it with all their followers, and some of them also share it to all their followers (and so on) it has the potential to create a cascade effect that reaches huge numbers of people.

But if the advertisement isn't done well, your own people probably won't think it worth sharing, and even if they do, it may not attract much interest. So it needs to be clear and accessible – and remember that almost certainly what works for a paper flyer might not work for a picture on social media. You need to think of the average user clicking and scrolling and think what would arrest their attention for a few seconds.

Another way to reach people who are not in your current set of church contacts is to have a go at social media advertising. This is, in effect, a paid campaign that targets a specific audience of social media users. It is not that expensive and gets around some of the algorithms that prevent most people other than your own followers from seeing your posts.

The only time we paid to advertise an event in our church, and it properly went viral, was when we did a 'Carols in the car park' during one of the Covid lockdowns in 2020. We did a bit of standard posting of the information with an option to book for the event (remember when we had to do that during the pandemic?). But then church members who had nothing better to do while being locked up at home started sharing it, which reached members of other churches, who also shared it – and then friends of friends started sharing as well. We ended up having to do three services in a row because of the demand! And it was cold... freezing cold.

So, your church needs to post something that will instantly provoke interest. And then you need members and friends of the church to 'like' and 'share'/'retweet' it, hopefully with an endorsing comment.

As individuals

There are many social media groups, or ad hoc chats on platforms like X (Twitter), where groups of Christians discuss issues. Some of these can be helpful, but most seem to me to be rather pointless and I wonder what on earth all their non-Christian friends think about it. I think they will likely conclude that Christians are just another political debating society.

I have also seen many Christian leaders using a secular model that builds a profile for themselves by constantly posting a combination of ministry and personal updates. That does seem to work for developing their likeability, but how evangelistic is it if it promotes the leader rather than Christ? Other Christian leaders constantly share other people's websites, which again is useful to other Christians, but not much help for outreach. Again, the question is, do you know what you are trying to achieve with your social media activity? If you want to make a difference for the gospel, then it has to inform and drive what you do and how you do it. Try to imagine your non-Christian friends and neighbours reading what you post. Let that guide you away from in-house squabbles and arrogant posturing, as well as dense writing full of Christian jargon and in-jokes.

The basic point I am making is this: churches should shift their social media messaging from proclaiming their church to proclaiming the gospel, and individuals should shift from sharing their lifestyles and personal achievements to sharing how the gospel is shaping their lives. Point people to Jesus, not to your church or yourself.[14]

Some dos and don'ts

Sadly, much of the posting by Christians on social media that I have seen seems to be sharing things of poor quality or displaying poor character. They post a notice of an event with no real thought about who will be reading it or how they are to respond. Or they write bad-tempered, self-indulgent tosh. Each platform works slightly differently, so try to think about what works well on the one you have chosen. Is it a longer or shorter comment? Is it short videos, or maybe photos on a theme? Think about who you are trying to reach and tailor the message accordingly.

Here are a few dos and don'ts:

- Do post things that will honour Christ, even if it is seemingly just about yourself and your new puppy (Col. 1:18). Don't post for all the world to see something that is essentially only of interest to your church or a network of people who already know you. Find another means of doing that.

14. https://fiec.org.uk/resources/3-ways-for-churches-to-creatively-use-social-media/ Accessed 12 December 2023.

- Do try and encourage a positive debate. Don't start a quarrel (Prov. 17:14).

- Do treat everyone like real people and afford them the same courtesy and grace that Christ would expect from you (Col. 4:2). Don't treat people like projects or debating opponents.

- Do be yourself. Don't try to be something you are not (2 Cor. 2:17).

- Do reflect on what you are going to say and listen carefully before answering. Don't post impulsively (Prov. 15:1).

- Do use social media to share good news. Don't use it to gossip, even if you might tell yourself it's spiritually profitable gossip (Prov. 20:19).

- Do be motivated by love in your posting and subsequent interactions. Don't be driven by pride, insecurity, anger, hatred, self-righteousness, boredom, a desire to control or to get back at someone.

- Do use social media to bring people together. Don't use it to stir up trouble or cause division.

- Do use it to commend the good (Eph. 4:29), to build up (1 Thess. 5:10-12), and say things that nourish (Prov. 10:21).

- Do sometimes say nothing at all! On social media, as in life, we sometimes need to avoid situations or people who gossip or cause us to become angry (Prov. 20:19). Don't boast or brag – actively by parading your own achievements or by the 'humble-brag' (pretending to be humble but in reality seeking the praise or comfort of others) (James 4:16).

Now you might say, and you would be correct, that all the above advice can just as easily apply to any area of our lives, not just social media. But that is the point: how we are in our online activity should reflect how we are in the rest of life. If you are a follower of Christ, and are being transformed by His Spirit into His likeness more and more each day, it should show in how you conduct yourself when you fire up Facebook or when you sit down at your keyboard to join in the conversation on the latest hot potato debate.

Be a Christian online, share your faith, and bring glory to God.

Questions for reflection and discussion

1. Write a mission statement for any Christian websites connected with your ministry or your church.

2. Think of some ideas for blogs or video shorts you could write and record. Try it out – go on!

3. Social media promotes inauthenticity because it allows us to create a curated, false version of ourselves online. How as Christians can we redeem our social media interactions?

Chapter 6

The Political Marketplace

'Defend the weak and the fatherless;
uphold the cause of the poor and the oppressed.
Rescue the weak and the needy;
deliver them from the hand of the wicked.'
(Psalm 82:3-4)

What is politics?

'Every compassionate Christian should oppose the government's proposed legislation on immigration. It's our moral duty. Why are Christians so silent on this?'

'Every sane Christian should be fully supportive of the government's approach to immigration because compassion has its limits and we have to consider its impact on other people in our care. It's not widows and orphans who are seeking sanctuary but mostly healthy young men who will exhaust our limited space and financial resources.'

'Christians should be at the forefront of anti-war demonstrations because all wars are immoral, and we should also be at the vanguard of environmental protests because we have a duty to protect the planet.'

'Christians should not be involved in politics; we should just preach the gospel. Changing the law will not save one single person.'

'No politician is worth voting for – and anyway politics is boring.'

'I cannot believe you voted for that party – they are a bunch of self-serving hypocrites.'

'We should be expending all our energy and political influence in trying to make the world a better place – that is how God's kingdom breaks in and redeems humanity.'

You will probably have heard all these views and more expressed by Christians. Should we be involved in politics? Is doing so part of fulfilling the Great Commission? Or should we keep well away from its murky waters? How do we decide our views on the important topics of the day and what is the best way to get started in doing some politicking (if we think it's a good idea at all).

What I want to try and persuade you about in this chapter is that politics in its broadest sense is something we need to get involved in, as part of our gospel outreach, and to give some ideas on how to do that. I acknowledge that Christianity and politics is a vast subject on which many good books have been written, so we will only be skimming the surface. Consider this as a bit of a taster session and you can get into the real meaty stuff in other publications.[15]

So what exactly is 'politics'? We might think of it as something that mainly happens in places like Westminster or the US Congress, far away from the life of the ordinary person in the street. It's all about battles for power, policy debates, intrigue, campaigning, name-calling, and how to avoid giving a straight answer to any question. It is not a highly valued profession. A recent survey by the Office for National Statistics in the UK showed that only 35 per cent of respondents trust our political parties and parliament. They identified five characteristics that can influence

---

15. A good place to start is Wayne Grudem, *Politics According to the Bible* (Zondervan, 2010).

trust: integrity, responsiveness, reliability, openness, and fairness.[1] Another poll conducted in 2022 found that belief in the truthfulness of politicians is down there with those other villains: estate agents and journalists. (Before we feel too smug, pastors come in only slightly better with just 55 per cent trusting them to tell the truth.)[2]

So, all things considered, should we really get involved in this dodgy business?

Let's go back to our new favourite city, Athens. The word the Greeks used for 'city' was *polis* and the citizens were *politēs*. Remember Aristotle? He was one of those famous Greek influencers who spent time in Athens as part of Plato's academy. It seems a lot of people there were almost permanent students. (We have some of those nowadays.) Anyway, Aristotle was what we would call these days a polymath – an expert in many fields of knowledge. (If you had to look up the word polymath then, like me, you're definitely not one.) He wrote about maths, logic, biology, physics, psychology, ethics, economics, poetry, rhetoric, and sport. In fact, I struggled to find anything he didn't write about. If he had his own podcast it would have run to more seasons than the Simpsons (which is thirty-four at the time of writing, to save you looking it up, and the children never grow up).

As far as we can tell it was Aristotle who first coined the word *politikos* when referring to the art or science of government. He wrote about how the *polis* (the city state) was governed and how the *politēs* (the citizens) interacted with it, and discussed what made for good laws and appropriate forms of government.

1. https://www.ons.gov.uk/peoplepopulationandcommunity/wellbeing/bulletins/trustingovernmentuk/2022. Accessed 12 December 2023.

2. https://www.ipsos.com/en-uk/ipsos-veracity-index-2022. Accessed 12 December 2023.

Some of the definitions he used are still applicable today and immediately recognisable in the world we live in. Here are some examples:

- *Monarchy* is a single person ruling as head of state for life or until abdication, usually to be replaced by a family member as rightful heir. While most monarchs would claim to rule for the common good, the system can tend towards tyranny.

- *Aristocracy* is rule by a small, privileged ruling class, whose authority and standing is hereditary, often passed from father to son.

- *Oligarchy* differs from aristocracy in that Aristotle saw this small group of leaders as being clearly motivated by selfish motives, often a desire for financial gain or power and influence for its own sake.

- *Democracy* is a system in which power lies in the hands of the people, who exercise their wishes through direct voting or by elected representatives. While most of us would consider this to be the best form of government, Aristotle disliked it. He considered that ordinary, uneducated people were gullible and easily influenced by corrupt despots or inclined to mob rule. (He may have a point.)

Interestingly, he believed that 'if a community contains an individual or family of outstanding excellence [then] monarchy is the best constitution. But such a case is very rare.'[3] I should say so!

Our democratic instincts might baulk at that idea of a monarch with unlimited powers, but think about it: If such a perfect ruler did exist, leading with complete

---

3. https://www.britannica.com/biography/Aristotle/Political-theory *Accessed 15 May 2023.*

justice and wisdom, would we not be happy? We could go about our daily lives, content in the knowledge that our affairs were in safe hands. In biblical history, maybe David came the closest to this ideal. We read in 2 Samuel 8:15 that, 'David reigned over all Israel, doing what was just and right for all his people'. Yet we know that he was also a deeply flawed individual.

The truly perfect king, Jesus Christ, would appear around three hundred years after Aristotle died. The eternal kingdom of God will not be a democracy, but it will be a place of perfect government, where we as citizens will be completely happy with our leader and our lives.

Meanwhile, we live in this world awaiting the appearing of that perfect existence. The Apostle Paul tells us that 'our citizenship is in heaven' (Phil. 3:20) but for now we live in this present age, under the rule of Christ but also as citizens here with roles and responsibilities. We are to 'shine like stars' in a warped world (Phil. 2:15). As we shall see in a moment, the gospel impacts the whole of life – including politics – but politics in the end will lead us back to the gospel, as we observe its limitations, because of our sinful tendencies, and we long for the perfect king.

In his survey of possible forms of government, Aristotle ends up proposing that a group of the elite should govern with the tacit consent of the people. It isn't exactly democracy but in practice it is probably closer than we care to admit to the form of government we actually have ourselves!

When we use the word politics in this book, we're talking about anything to do with the way we organise and make laws or rules to govern everything, from the village fete to the nation state to the world powers; from potholes to tax rates to pandemics, natural disasters, and war.

Should we do politics?

It is probably a bit of a stretch to say that Paul would have been talking about local politics in the agora at Athens. His priority on mission was to preach Christ (1 Cor. 2:2). But as a well-read Roman citizen, he would certainly have been aware of the political situation wherever he went. The agora was a place where local justice was enacted and no doubt debated, so it is hard to believe that politics never came up in his daily discussions in the market.

As we saw in chapter one, Paul's sermon to the Areopagus displays his knowledge of relatively obscure Greek poets. In writing to Titus, he shows awareness of popular national stereotypes and quotes another poet in Crete (Titus 1:12). Being so well read, it thus seems certain that he would also have read some of Plato, Aristotle, and the like. Some scholars claim to detect allusions to both philosophers in Acts 17 and in virtually all his letters that we have in the New Testament.[4]

In addition, Paul taught about the important role of the state (Romans 13), and he spoke truth to those in power as he defended himself against wrongful arrest before the Roman governor Felix (Acts 24:25). Paul's political philosophy was shaped by the Bible and the teachings of Christ. The principles he lays out for us may not tell us how to vote in an election but we have in his writings and in the rest of Scripture much that we can use to inform our thinking as we exercise our democratic rights and engage in the political process.

Rulers are established by God

As Paul writes in Romans 13, 'the powers', whether they be on a throne, in a national parliament or local town

---

4. https://biblethingsinbibleways.wordpress.com/2013/07/14/paul-and-his-use-of-greek-philosophy/ *for a detailed analysis.* Accessed 12 December 2023.

hall, are placed there by God. As Daniel prayed when he was about to confront Nebuchadnezzar, the supreme earthly ruler of his day, 'Praise be to the name of God for ever and ever; wisdom and power are his. He changes times and seasons; he deposes kings and raises up others' (Dan. 2:20-21). Then later, when he stands before the party-loving Babylonian king Belshazzar to interpret the writing on the wall he says, 'God is sovereign over all kingdoms on earth and sets over them anyone he wishes' (Dan. 5:21).

A few years ago we enjoyed watching Kiefer Sutherland playing Tom Kirkman in the TV drama series *Designated Survivor*. An explosion destroys the Capitol building in Washington, killing the President and everyone in the line of succession except for Kirkman, the Secretary of Housing and Urban Development, a fairly minor government role filled by a less than impressive character.

This insignificant politician had been named the 'designated survivor' – the one member of the government to be kept away from major events in case of an attack wiping out everyone else. And thus Kirkman is immediately sworn in. He is very much the accidental President – the one who was never meant to be in power; the one no one expected or wanted.

But with God there are no accidental leaders. All of them, the good, the bad, and the downright terrible, are raised up by God whether they achieve power by an apparent accident of history, bloodline, war, revolution, or the ballot box. And they remain in position until God says it's time for them to be deposed and at that point nothing will keep them in office one moment longer.

Political power is God's way of restraining evil

Paul writes to Christians living in Rome – the seat of political power in the empire – and reminds them that

'The authorities that exist have been established by God' (Rom. 13:1). He then describes God's purpose in their appointment to rule: '...the one in authority is God's servant for your good. But if you do wrong, be afraid, for rulers do not bear the sword for no reason' (Rom. 13:4). Again, the Apostle Peter writes that the authorities are there to '...punish those who do wrong and commend those who do right' (1 Pet. 2:14). Even despotic leaders have a role in restraining evil.

What this means is that governments, even the most corrupt or tyrannical, are in some way – maybe known only to God – fulfilling a role in restraining the evil that would spiral out of control if there were no laws and no enforcement. They are part of God's order. This is not to say that all governments are good and should never be replaced. Clearly some are more evil than others and may eventually suffer their just reward, but nonetheless God places them in power for His purposes.

We submit to political powers out of respect for God

Recognising that God has given political power, it is therefore right for us to submit to that authority, giving honour and respect to those in power – and that includes paying our taxes! We do this even when the party we voted for doesn't win. We honour the hosepipe bans, pandemic restrictions, frustrating 20mph speed limits, and many other rules that we don't necessarily agree with, because we recognise God's ultimate purpose. When we honour them, we are not saying they are perfect, or that we give our unqualified approval of all that they do. We do so out of fear and reverence for God. As Peter goes on to say: '... fear God, honour the emperor' (1 Pet. 2:17).

The only exception to this stance of submission seems to be when to obey would be to sin and dishonour God.

So, for example, when Peter was forbidden to preach the gospel by the Jewish authorities, he replied, 'We must obey God rather than human beings!' (Acts 5:29).

As Francis Schaeffer writes: 'When any *office* commands that which is contrary to the Word of God, those who hold that office abrogate their authority and they are not to be obeyed. And that includes the state... God has ordained the state as a delegated authority; it is not autonomous. The state is to be an agent of justice, to restrain evil by punishing the wrongdoer, and to protect the good in society. When it does the reverse, it has no proper authority. It is then a usurped authority and as such it becomes lawless and is tyranny.'[5]

This does not imply that we have an excuse to rebel against any law of the land that we happen to disagree with. Some Christians on social media seem to me to be much too ready to denigrate their political opponents, especially those in power. In Acts 5, obedience to the authorities required disobedience to God; we cannot extrapolate from that to situations today which are far less black-and-white, which require wisdom and judgment, and in which Christians may genuinely disagree as to what the correct response should be.

Of course, we can campaign against policies we believe to be wrong; that is our democratic right – but we submit to the law even as we seek to get it changed. This is a vital principle for our political engagement – we do it humbly and submissively. We should speak about our leaders with respect even when we disagree.

So we should pray for our leaders to rule well in the way God intended – to reward righteous behaviour and punish evil. We should also pray for good leaders to be appointed at election time. At the same time, whatever the party in power, we must also live well as good citizens as we

---

5. Schaeffer, Francis A., *A Christian Manifesto* (Crossway, 2005), pp. 90-91

honour God, the King, the government, the magistrate, the traffic warden, and the school teacher.

We pray for our politicians for the sake of gospel witness

We also pray for our leaders. Paul, writing to Timothy, urged that prayers, intercessions and thanksgiving be made for 'all people' and then he singles out 'kings and those in authority' (1 Tim. 2:2). The goal of our prayer is 'that we may live peaceful and quiet lives in all godliness and holiness'. This doesn't mean we pray for an easy life! It seems to me that this means we pray for order and safety in society so that we will have a stable environment in which to preach the gospel. This does not mean we cannot witness when society is falling apart – sometimes this provides even greater opportunities for God's Word to be heard; but in general we can best take advantage of gospel freedoms when the rule of law is upheld.

Politics is a different sphere to the kingdom of God

In Matthew 22 Jesus was approached by a group that included some junior Pharisees and the Herodians. As their name suggests the Herodians were supporters of King Herod, and in turn generally doing rather well out of the Roman empire. After some weasel words by way of introduction they ask a simple but politically loaded question: 'Is it right to pay the poll tax to Caesar or not?' (Matt. 22:17). It seems a straightforward question but, in fact, it was a trap.

In 1990, the UK Prime Minister Margaret Thatcher introduced the Community Charge to England and Wales, a new way of collecting taxes to pay for local services, which came to be known as the poll tax. It was hugely controversial because it was a flat-rate charge on every adult, set by the local authority, regardless of where they lived and how many people they lived with, which appeared to discriminate against the poor. Its introduction led to widespread demonstrations and rioting on a level that took the government by surprise.

In Roman-occupied Israel in the first century, the poll tax was even more hated as it represented a levy on the subject peoples and was a constant reminder of their subservient status. So if Jesus had answered, 'Yes, you should pay the tax', He would have appeared to be an unpatriotic Jew. The Pharisees could then brand Him a traitor to His people. If he had said 'No', then the Herodians, who supported Roman rule, could have accused Him of being a revolutionary zealot and reported Him to the Romans who would have locked Him up.

So it was a clever question, designed to force Jesus into condemning Himself by His own words, one way or another. In order to wriggle out of the trap, Jesus might have chosen the modern politician's ploy of ignoring the question; instead He answers them in a most remarkable way with words that have echoed down the centuries and been quoted countless times.

He asked to be shown a coin. The local currency was minted by the Romans and so when he asked whose image and inscription it bore they answered, 'Caesar's'. The portrait was that of Caesar Augustus Tiberius, stepson of the previous Caesar (also called Augustus, just to confuse us all). This first Augustus was designated a god when he died, so the inscription in full would have said 'son of the Divine Augustus'. So this coin, which they would have used to pay the hated poll tax, also trumpeted the blasphemous claims of their occupying rulers. What was Jesus going to say?

I expect you could have heard a pin drop. Then Jesus spoke with words so simple and yet so profound that it sent everyone away amazed – words which are the foundation for how Christians have related to the kingdom of God and the kingdoms of this world ever since: 'Give back to Caesar what is Caesar's, and to God what is God's.'

In other words, they should give to Caesar what is rightfully his. Despite what the Jews felt so deeply, Caesar really did carry authority in their land. However corrupt and idolatrous he may have been, he was to be given respect, and had the right to levy taxes, which were thus to be paid.

However, we might say, that is only one side of the coin! Jesus declared that God must also be given what is rightfully His. And what is that? God's imprint is stamped on the whole world; hHis image is seen in every human being. We all belong to Him. Thus, our highest allegiance is to God. And what this meant was that, in demanding to be worshipped, a Roman emperor was seeking more than his due.

In all of life there are various spheres of activity with their own networks of rule and authority. The family is one such very significant and fundamental example. And, like the family, the government has a role to play and a sphere of authority in God's economy. But ultimately it is God Himself who stands as the supreme overarching authority and it is His Word in Scripture that regulates and shapes all lower spheres of authority, informing them as to what is good, righteous, wise, true, and just.

What these words of Jesus mean for the church is that we must be a community of people who live in this world in such a way that we honour our 'kings' on earth, living as good citizens, but also never forgetting that our supreme allegiance is to our heavenly Lord.

This separation of what belongs to Caesar and what belongs to God has important implications for church-state relations. It implies that the state should not interfere with, or seek to dictate, what a church believes or how it practises its faith. We accept the need for churches to comply with all manner of standards and laws regarding such things as health and safety, finances, safeguarding, building regulations, and so on. Individual church members are also subject to the civil and criminal law of the land. But according to Jesus, the state oversteps its God-given authority if it tries to influence or dictate what the church believes, preaches, teaches, or prays.

Politics is an outworking of our discipleship

Some might say that we really should not get involved in politics as Christians. They would argue, quite rightly, that preaching the gospel and making disciples is our priority. They could correctly point out that neither Jesus nor His followers formed a political party to challenge the Pharisees, or started an insurrection against the occupying forces of the Romans. On the contrary, Jesus explicitly told Peter to put his sword away when he tried to prevent Jesus being arrested (John 18:11). Then, during His trial, Jesus told Pilate, 'My kingdom is not of this world' (John 18:36).

There certainly is a clear call from Jesus to seek first God's kingdom (Matt. 6:33). We calibrate all our other worries and concerns against the priority of being in the kingdom and growing in the likeness of Christ.

John MacArthur writes, 'Jesus did not come to earth to make the old creation moral through social and governmental reform but to make new creatures holy through the saving power of the gospel and transforming work of the Holy Spirit.'[6] I agree with that, but would still say that, properly understood, seeking first the kingdom will include some politics! If we are to follow the Great Commission and teach and do everything Jesus

6. MacArthur, John, *Why Government Can't Save You* (Zondervan, 2000), p. 8

commanded, this will have implications for our parenting, our workplace relationships, our finances, our leisure time – and how we relate to the governing powers, both local and national.

In his book, *Gospel Witness*, Joe Boot writes, 'Our witness to the truth involves much more than simply sharing our testimony of personal salvation and forgiveness of sins – it includes this but surely encapsulates the totality of our renewed lives and Christ's redemptive purposes for the whole cosmos... the practical application of the gospel for people to see the Lord reigns.'[7] It is also how we work out the command to love our neighbours. We want the best for other people in society and so we want good laws that will reward the good, punish the bad, and protect the weak. Let me try and illustrate it like this: suppose a child in a family of unbelievers becomes a Christian. That child will of course want their whole family to become Christians. But that child will also wish its parents to order their family life differently, providing a new, clearer moral framework that protects and directs all their children. Why? Because the new believer wants the best for the family. In the same way, we should not be indifferent about the state of our nation but want its laws to protect and direct all members for their good.

As we teach the whole counsel of God (Acts 20:27) it will impact politics as it will evangelism. Wayne Grudem says, '...the *do evangelism not politics* view has a mistaken understanding of what is important to God, as if only spiritual things matter to him and not the actual circumstances of people's physical life in this world.'[8] Or to put it another way, which parts of the Bible shall we not preach about or put into practice in order to avoid

---

7. Boot, Joseph, *Gospel Witness* (Wilberforce Publications, 2017), p. 119
8. Grudem, p. 47

politics? We will end up with a very slimmed down Word of God.

In some way or other, whether as obedient, prayerful citizens or as active participants in the governing process, we should be engaged in doing politics; the only questions are where and how we will be doing so. It is a good and Christian thing to play an active role in the structures God has ordained for society's ordering and security, an order that includes, for example, caring for the weak and also holding back the tide of evil. Politics is not how we get salvation but is part of how we work it out 'with fear and trembling' (Phil. 2:12).

As with every human endeavour, we need to be careful that it doesn't become an idol. We may become so engrossed in the political process, enjoying the cut and thrust of debate, and the thrill of influencing policy, that we forget first things. If people coming to faith in Christ becomes less important to us than political power, something has gone wrong. We need to be realistic about the limits of political goals. In one sense, all political careers end in failure so we 'do not trust in princes' (Ps. 146:3). As Christians we are not seeking salvation through politics. We are extending the rule of God and His claim over the laws we make, but ultimately, as Ian Paul writes, 'the business of human politics in the midst of history is about holding back as best we can the sweeping tide of human evil. Government is a practical, even pragmatic, art – often the art of deciding between the lesser of many evils, with incomplete or inaccurate knowledge. Human rulers are as sinful as those they govern.'[9]

So we should engage with politics at some level as our gifts and opportunities allow, and both speak truth

---

9. https://www.psephizo.com/life-ministry/how-should-christians-engage-in-politics/ Accessed 12 December 2023.

to power and exercise influence in a way that is an outworking of our following of Christ. If you live in a democracy then you have a degree of power through the voting system. One way in which we show love for our neighbour is to take seriously the responsibility to use our vote wisely. We will want to elect a government that works for the good of all. Governments significantly reflect but also influence the moral convictions and behaviour of a nation.[10] If we don't use our vote, others will and their influence may not tend to righteousness.

While we cannot use politics to bring about God's kingdom on earth, we can work for policies that help the poor, the sick, the elderly, and others who are in need. We can work to protect the environment and promote peace and to ensure that governments and their laws reflect our values of love, compassion, and justice. We can also work to oppose laws and policies that are harmful to others. We are called to 'Speak up for those who cannot speak for themselves, for the rights of all who are destitute. Speak up and judge fairly; defend the rights of the poor and needy' (Prov. 31:8-9). There is a personal obligation for our own acts of charity and advocacy and for what we can do as a church to help the needy but, almost certainly, as we are dealing with groups of people not personally known to us, it is something we will do in the political sphere.

Some of this working out of our following Jesus and all that He commanded might be as a servant of the government. Looking at Scripture, we have great examples of people who used their positions of influence to work for the good of the people:

- There was Joseph, working in Egypt. He was sold into slavery by his jealous brothers, unfairly accused by Potiphar's wife, and unjustly imprisoned, yet he

---

10.   Grudem, p. 97

ended up as the Prime Minister under Pharoah, saving many lives from famine across Egypt and preserving the family of his father Jacob.

• Daniel was taken captive as a young man to Babylon and became a prominent civil servant under three kings (more of him in a moment).

• Plucked from obscurity as a young Jewish woman, Esther became the wife of the Persian King Xerxes. Her cousin and guardian Mordecai also served in some role in the court of the king and as such was able to foil an assassination plot against Xerxes. Later, when the Jewish people were under threat of extinction, Esther spoke up bravely on their behalf and brought about their salvation.

All three of these Old Testament believers were faithful servants under a tyrannical regime. They served their pagan masters well, but refused to compromise when their ultimate loyalty to God was put to the test.

When we come to the New Testament, we see Christians in positions of secular authority such as Cornelius, a Roman centurion in the Italian Regiment. He was a 'God-fearer' prior to his conversion in Acts 10 and we have no reason to think that he resigned his position after following Christ. Zacchaeus was a corrupt tax collector before he met Jesus (Luke 19:1-10) but we are not told that Jesus asked him to abandon his profession. However, his new faith meant that from then on he would live by a different code of ethics, without exploiting the poor for his own gain.

All these characters were living by faith and living out their faith as they sought to be both good servants to their earthly rulers and also an influence for good where they served. Each had to navigate a difficult pagan culture, balancing their duties to God and Caesar.

In more recent history, William Wilberforce (1759–1833), an English politician and devout Christian, campaigned tirelessly for the abolition of slavery, driven by his Christian beliefs and conviction of the inherent worth and dignity of every human being.

Robert Raikes (1735–1811) influenced prison reform and set up Sunday schools. At this time upper-class children were taught at home by tutors, middle-class children might go to a local grammar school but children of the poor worked six days a week and received no education to speak of. Raikes wanted them to read, write, and learn mathematics. His work was also motivated by a desire that they should hear the gospel and be able to read the Bible for themselves. His legacy led to the provision of education for all children.

Frederic Rainer (1836–1911) was a printer and member of the *Church of England Temperance Society* who donated five shillings to the *Church of England Temperance Society* to create the Police Court Missions, who gave advice and support to criminal offenders coming out of prison, and helped them with jobs and independent living. This eventually formed the basis of our modern-day probation service.[11]

While these and many other Christians in public life made headlines and are still known to us today, many more ordinary believers have worked, and continue to work, faithfully in the secular sphere, as an influence both for good and for the gospel, locally and nationally. Their discipleship is seen in lives out in the world, not hidden away in holy huddles.

---

11. https://rootbranchexhibition.wordpress.com/five-shillings/ Accessed 12 December 2023.

Politics is part of our witness to the nations

Have you ever wondered why significant parts of the writings of the Old Testament prophets are addressed to nations other than Israel? Israel was to be light to the nations – how they conducted their life and worship was to be a witness to other peoples who did not know the Lord. But all nations are ultimately under God's rule and just as Israel faced the denunciations of the prophets for their sin, so too did their neighbours.

So the book of Amos begins with the LORD 'roaring' from Zion, calling out the nations for their conduct. His call to Judah to 'hate evil, love good; maintain justice in the courts' (Amos 5:15) is required by all peoples. Isaiah 13–23; Jeremiah 46–51; Ezekiel 25–32; Obadiah, Nahum, Habakkuk 2, and Zephaniah are all directed at the surrounding nations – a testimony to the concern the LORD has for justice and truth in the whole world.

Having noted all this, it would be a mistake to lift it into the New Covenant era and conclude that the Christian church should seek to impose biblical law on nation states, including our own. Israel was a theocracy, with a relationship to God's law like no other state. So what role, if any, should Old Testament law play in contemporary political debate?

Some theologians divide the law into three categories:

- *Ceremonial law* – the sacrificial system centred on the desert tabernacle and, later, the Jerusalem temple.

- *Moral law* – basically the Ten Commandments (Exodus 20) but also developed and worked out in many other places.

- *Civil law* – that which codifies the application of the Ten Commandments into detailed rules for the national life of Israel.

There is some debate around whether those categories are useful but, in terms of their relevance for today, all would agree that the ceremonial law is now obsolete and at an end. This complex array of offerings and rituals pointed forward to Christ – the Lamb of God who has taken away the sins of the world (John 1:29) – and thus has been fulfilled in Him. There is also in the New Testament no expectation in the words of Jesus or the apostles that the authorities are obliged to follow the detailed civil laws imposed on Israelite society.

However, when we consider the moral law – as summarised in the Ten Commandments – we see a standard of morality and ethics that applies not just to a particular time, place, or other set of circumstances, but that reflects the unchanging character of God Himself. Thus we should recognise a responsibility not just to an appropriation of these commandments into our individual lives and the life of the church (the new Israel), but also their application to wider community life.

So, for example, if we think that God calls us to preserve life: 'You shall not murder' (Exod. 20:13), we will want the law of our land to reflect that standard. If the God of Israel required equity: 'But let justice roll on like a river' (Amos 5:24) then we will want our courts and civil laws to uphold fairness for all. As God required generous treatment of the weak and vulnerable – 'Do no wrong or violence to the foreigner, the fatherless or the widow' (Jer. 22:3) – then surely we would want our government to legislate for the same? If we believe that God condemns adultery and sexual immorality: 'You shall not commit adultery' (Exod. 20:14), we would want to obey Him personally – but wouldn't we also want laws that encourage Christian marriage, amongst other things?

Take the case of Daniel. He exercised a significant influence on the secular government of Babylon and the

Medo-Persian empire. Here he was in an alien culture being a responsible civil servant – doing politics. Did he agree with every law of the land? Surely not. Did he have days in work when he had to grapple with his conscience over how to respond to the expectations placed upon him as a servant of the state? Absolutely; we know he did. And yet such was his integrity and faithfulness to his employer that he was promoted over and over again. His reputation was outstanding; even his enemies '...could find no corruption in him, because he was trustworthy and neither corrupt nor negligent' (Dan. 6:4).

Such was his character in the royal court that when the opportunity came to speak truth to power, Daniel was courageous enough to take it and the mighty Nebuchadnezzar was ready to listen: 'Therefore, Your Majesty, be pleased to accept my advice: Renounce your sins by doing what is right, and your wickedness by being kind to the oppressed. It may be that then your prosperity will continue' (Dan. 4:27). Daniel was a believer exercising 'significant influence on a civil government ruled by a pagan king'.[12]

What about John the Baptist calling out the sin of Herod (Luke 3:18-20)? He, too, used his platform as a notable individual – although certainly no court favourite! – to speak truth to power.

Neither was the Apostle Paul an establishment figure by the time his own people had turned against him for preaching Christ (Gal. 1:23). But he, too, was unafraid to address the moral failings of the powerful. On his way to trial in Rome, Paul addressed Felix, the Roman procurator of Judea, described by the Roman historian Tacitus as 'cruel, licentious, and base'. As Paul 'talked about righteousness, self-control and the judgment to come, Felix was afraid and said, "That's enough for now!

---

12. Grudem, p. 59

You may leave"' (Acts 24:25). So it is very likely that as well as telling his own story, Paul also called Felix to account for his ruthless conduct as an imperial official.[13]

So what about us? We can speak the gospel to politicians, but more than that we can also speak about how God's good and righteous laws are for our good and for our flourishing, and that when we ignore them we are likely to suffer all sorts of necessary consequences.

Justice and fairness matter to God. We cannot be indifferent about whether the government has an equitable immigration or benefit system, or whether the legal system punishes the wrongdoer and provides justice for those who have been wronged. Because we are guided by God's law, we have an opinion about the rich exploiting the poor. The nobles in Nehemiah's day were charging 1 per cent interest and were condemned for their exploitation (Neh. 5:1-11). Charging interest is not wrong in itself, but Scripture condemns the rich getting richer at the expense of the poor or leveraging their power to exploit the poor. Another prophet described Israel as those who 'defraud labourers of their wages, who oppress the widows and the fatherless, and deprive the foreigners among you of justice' (Mal. 3:5).

It matters that we have a system that treats people fairly; it matters how our rulers treat the vulnerable. Being involved in politics is a way for Christians to live out their faith and to be a voice for God's justice and truth to permeate all levels of society. We can be a light to the nations as we share our faith with others and show them how it can be applied in the public square. We can use our political involvement to challenge the culture and point people to Christ. We can call out sin and seek to stir the conscience of others. In the mercy of God, it might lead to better, more just and compassionate government, but

---

13. Grudem, p. 35

also provide a living and concrete demonstration of the character of God – His truth and righteousness – and give opportunities to show others how they might come to know this God through the gospel of His Son.

How can you get involved in politics?

I hope that by now I might have been able to convince you that every Christian has a duty to get involved in politics in some form or another, from simply acting as a responsible citizen to serving in some form of local or national civic organisation.

For some of us, this might mean we get more directly involved in influencing policy, being salt and light, doing good, bringing God's wisdom into public discourse and, in so doing, provoking the sort of questions that would never otherwise be raised. I recognise that this will not be for all of us, but surely it must be for some of us! Do we really want to vacate this space, leaving it completely for those with either a secular agenda or other religious affiliations to decide how our society and nation is ordered? Is that a responsible thing to do?

Some will respond that as long as we are faithful in preaching the gospel, we are fulfilling the call of Christ to His church. But His teaching includes the command to love our neighbours as ourselves (Matt. 22:39). I hope I have demonstrated that this requires much more than telling them about Christ, even though this is their greatest need.

Assuming that you have come thus far with me in my reasoning, you may be wondering how to start engaging in political activity. Here are some ideas to get you going:

Be a good citizen

Step one of applying the Bible's teaching about politics is to be the kind of citizen, neighbour, and community activist that God is calling you to be and that Jesus modelled for you.

Obey those in authority generously and cheerfully, not grudgingly. Be known as someone who can be trusted and who is honest and even-handed in all your dealings. Remember what Daniel's enemies discovered: 'They could find no corruption in him, because he was trustworthy and neither corrupt nor negligent', concluding that 'We will never find any basis for charges against this man Daniel unless it has something to do with the law of his God' (Dan. 6:4-5).

Connect with your local political leaders. Don't just contact them when you have something to complain about – show yourself to be constructive and supportive; they will take note of this as not many people are! Ask what their most pressing issues are at the moment and how you can help. Say that you are praying for them and make it your practice to do so regularly as part of your daily devotions. Let your elected officials know about the issues that are important to you. You can write a letter, email, text, phone, or even visit them in person at their surgeries.

Vote

This is one of the most obvious ways to participate in politics for most us who live in democratic nations. It is something we can all do.

Some Christians think we should not vote on principle, as to do so is to participate in 'the world'. This misapplies the separation that Scripture calls Christians to observe. Remember Jesus' lesson from the Roman coin: we participate in two spheres of authority. Our ultimate duty is to our heavenly master, but we are also citizens of this world. That being so, we pay our taxes and show honour to Caesar – and we also vote.

You might think that your vote doesn't really count because of the dominance of one particular party in your local constituency. However, by responsibly quizzing the candidates at an election and casting your vote you are making your voice heard. Try to elect those who will best represent righteous values. I know that for many Christians in the Western world, this can be a pretty depressing exercise because on some moral issues none of the candidates will represent your views. So you must try to weigh up the many policies on offer and try to decide which you believe most reflect Christian values (or least contradict them!).

You may wish to weigh up not just the parties represented, but also the personal character and views of each individual candidate. Maybe one of them has served the constituency faithfully and with great diligence in the last parliament; maybe he or she has been willing to stand up for a righteous cause in defiance of the parliamentary party; maybe he or she has interacted very positively with you on some issue of concern. Should these considerations tip the balance in favour of this person despite the fact that you would not normally vote for that party? Or does the fact that the national party is standing on a platform that seems to be so hostile to your faith make it impossible to vote this way?

Making such decisions is not an easy task! We are trying to take Christian principles and apply them to specific policies and ideologies. This is further complicated by the fact that modern politics is as much about personalities as about policies, and if a party has a coherent ideology it is not always easy to spot. All this means that we may end up disagreeing with other Christians about our voting intentions. If that is so, we should disagree without rancour or bitterness.

Serve your locality

There are plenty of community and political issues for you to get stuck into locally. Find out what issues affect your neighbours. Can you find a common cause to work with them on? Can you make a noise about key issues local to you? Is there a community organisation you can help to lead? Could you become a trustee or a governor at a local school or college? You might start a debt advice service or foodbank, or run some other kind of community project – maybe a café? Do the local youth or old people's services need volunteers? You might think of these as social action matters, which they are, but they are also local people, sometimes local authorities, operating in the interest and for the benefit of its citizens. Aristotle called it politics.

Get a job

Part of your good citizenship might be that you seek employment in a department of local or national government. Even as an unelected officer you can be salt and light. The more senior the role, the more obviously you can also influence policy. But at any level you may improve the 'religious literacy' of government. The Bloom Review which reported in April 2023, inquired into the ways in which government engages with 'faith'. The review showed that 'many respondents think faith engagement among some government institutions and public agencies needs improvement'.[14] As society has become increasingly secular, so government departments and their officials have a growing difficulty in understanding the significant minority of people in the UK who have a strong faith that shapes their motivations and attitudes. Your role may be

---

14.   *Does government 'do God'? An independent review into how government engages with faith.* https://assets.publishing.service.gov.uk/government/uploads/system/uploads/attachment_data/file/1152684/The_Bloom_Review.pdf. Accessed 12 December 2023.

to help educate your colleagues and give them a greater respect and knowledge of what a Christian believes, both about the gospel and every other matter.

Get elected

Another obvious way to get more directly involved in politics is to run for office. To do so you will probably have to start locally; Prime Minister or President is probably not quite within your reach this week, but we all have to start somewhere.

Being an elected representative is a way to have a direct impact on matters that affect people's lives. It might be that you can use your position to argue for greater help for vulnerable children or for keeping open a day centre for adults with learning difficulties. On a more mundane level you might help to get those potholes fixed more quickly!

If you don't want to run for office yourself, you can still help with the local party organisation. This may mean canvassing for a candidate at a local or national election, or volunteering at the campaign office. Find out about and join the Christian group within the party of your choice (they all have one) and be an advocate for what you believe Jesus' politics would require of their policies.

Be an advocate for others

Whether in political office, or as a campaigner, you can stand up and make your voice heard by lawmakers on the issues of the day. The priority should be to speak up for those who do not have a voice, to use our individual and organised power to love our neighbours.

Be aware it might get messy. Sometimes you may have to compromise in order to get things done; you may need to work with non-Christians and nominal Christians in common cause. Great wisdom will be needed to weigh up the issues.

Here are some areas where you might want to comment and campaign:

International poverty and human rights

All across the world there are people facing starvation. A variety of factors are involved, some natural (weather, crop failure) but many others are of human origin (civil war, corruption etc.). Other people are persecuted minorities in their own lands, and many are denied the right to just and fair treatment by their courts. We cannot speak up for all of them, of course, and we may be far removed from having much influence, but we do need to take some of the opportunities presented to us to ask our government to get involved. They could put diplomatic and maybe even economic pressure on these nations to stop their breaches of human rights.

The right to life

Both in our own country and in many others as well, the sacredness of human existence, especially at the beginning and end of life, is under threat as never before. Who will speak up for these defenceless ones? While it has been legal in the UK since 1967, we must not give up campaigning against abortion.

Also in the UK there is a powerful and vocal lobby pushing for assisted suicide to be legalised. If this were to succeed, it is to be feared that many vulnerable people will feel themselves under pressure, real or perceived, to end their lives prematurely. Where this has been enacted in other nations, it is often not just the terminally ill who are affected, but the lonely, the mentally ill, and those living with disabilities and chronic health conditions. Some might feel obliged to end their lives to relieve the burden on family and friends.

The greater need is to see more and better palliative care available for those in the latter stages of life. Assisted suicide could otherwise become the cheap alternative to properly funding end-of-life and social care. Do we want those with disabilities, mental illness, or other long-term problems to be forced to choose death because there is no help for them to live?[15]

We should also advocate for a fairer system of welcoming refugees to our nation whose lives are under threat. While we should probably accept that we cannot accommodate all who want to come, we must not give in to those who would turn most people away. We should also be supportive of efforts to address the roots of the problem of international refugees, and the fight against all forms of modern slavery.

Social and economic policy

In the area of economics, and the way government revenues are raised and how they are spent, Bible-believing Christians have different viewpoints, all sincerely held. Recognising this fact should mean not that we refuse to debate it but that we do so with a good measure of mutual respect. It should also moderate the way we put forward our arguments and how we listen to alternative positions. It is healthy and helpful to reflect on what we think about wealth and the welfare state, about taxes and profits, about redistribution of wealth, and the huge divide that exists between the haves and the have-nots.

For example, someone will argue that in order to be generous to others, we have to generate that wealth in the first place. Thus, government policy, including taxation, should encourage enterprise and business. Others will complain that wealth should not be a goal for its own

15. https://www.affinity.org.uk/social-issues/assisted-dying-is-society-giving-up-on-the-vulnerable/ Accessed 12 December 2023.

sake and that it is the role of government to have more control over the means of production in order to promote fairer ways of both wealth creation and its redistribution to the most needy in society. Christians will take different positions on these matters and each will believe they have done so for the best of reasons.

So often in these wider debates people argue from positions of self-interest. What is in it for me? Which party will give me more spending power if it comes to power? Will this party or that preserve my privileges and my way of life? For the Christian, this way of thinking is not an option. We must advocate for the benefit of others if they are more needy.

For example, if you own the property you live in, would you work for the rights of those in private rented accommodation and social housing? Would you campaign for better drug dependency and mental health services, even if nobody you know needs such help? It is known that black households are the most likely to be living in poverty, in areas of deprivation, on low income, with higher rates of unemployment and in single parent families.[16] If you are not an ethnic minority yourself, are you willing to be challenged by these statistics and to join with others in seeking to advocate for them, to support research into the causes and efforts to change things?

Family

We need to speak up about the importance of marriage as taught in the Bible. We should call for age-appropriate sex education in schools and for it to be set within the context of a broader understanding of morality, including an explanation of what Christians (and most world religions) believe on this subject.

---

16. https://manifesto.nclf.org.uk/dl/Articles/m/83abeb/r/QnfIERJAS4uY31N1Epxa6A. Accessed 12 December 2023.

In 2023 there was a survey in England of 1,100 sixteen to eighteen year-olds, particularly on issues of sex and relationship education.[17] Some of the findings included:

- One in ten of those surveyed wanted to change their gender or had already done so.

- Nearly a third said that they had been taught that a woman can have a penis while one in five said they had learnt that a man can get pregnant.

- Almost a quarter said that sex education lessons had included details on bondage, domination, and sadomasochism.

- Four in ten said they had learnt that young men were a problem in society and a similar number were told Britain was a structurally racist country.

- A third said different viewpoints were encouraged by the school but they did not feel confident sharing their views. A sixth said their school had taught a single viewpoint.

- More than half of pupils supported lowering the age of a gender recognition certification from eighteen to sixteen.

On the wider issue of transgenderism, Christians believe that our gender is fixed by God as He orders the circumstances of our conception, and that it is neither good nor healthy to change our gender presentation, characteristics, or genitals. We have great compassion for those who struggle with gender confusion but do not think that the best way to support them is to affirm them in a lie, but rather to help them live as their given gender without needing to conform to gender stereotypes.

---

17. https://civitas.org.uk/content/files/Show-tell-and-leave-nothing-to-the-imagination-.pdf. Accessed 12 December 2023.

Of particular concern in this report are issues to do with exposing children to ideas about gender, sexuality, and sex that are inappropriate at a time when their brains and emotional maturity are still developing. The problem is not with teaching the fact of different sexual relationships and the people who might choose to live in a way that contradicts their biology, but it is the level of detail that they are receiving, with no discussion of alternative views on these topics.

It is perfectly reasonable to seek to be an advocate for children by challenging your school or college on the level of detail that is being given and for them to not teach opinion as fact. For example, it has not been established in science or agreed in society that a child can be 'born in the wrong body'. This is a contested issue across the board, not just by Christians. Some of the teaching they are receiving on this subject may itself be a form of unwanted sexual exposure and pressure, which, in other contexts, might be considered abusive. We should thus be encouraging schools to allow all opinions on ethical issues, not just one socially liberal view. We can of course offer to put forward the Christian perspective if they need someone to do so.

Likewise, most of the UK governments want to ban 'practices' that seek to 'change, suppress or inhibit' someone's sexual orientation or gender identity. If enacted, church leaders and ordinary Christians who engage in normal pastoral ministry and prayer, and parents talking to their own children, may find themselves on the wrong side of the law. We need to make a stand against such proposals, not just for our sake, but for the good of society as a whole.

The environment

Some Christians, for scientific and theological reasons, oppose some of the current climate change catastrophising as being disproportionate and because it seems to have its roots in a form of neo-pagan, pantheistic worship of 'mother earth'. Whatever your views on the science and the politics – whether you believe we should stop burning fossil fuels today, or you think climate science is voodoo – there is plenty of common ground we can make with environmentalists.

For example, while we certainly do not apologise for our presence on the earth, we do recognise the need to reduce the amount of waste we create that goes into landfill. This is God's creation and our faithful stewardship of the resources He has given to us means we need to address pollution and support policies that promote biodiversity.

Most of us will probably not want to stop using all mechanical transport and go back to walking and horses, but we do recognise the problem of air pollution as it particularly affects young children, pregnant women, the elderly, and people suffering from heart and lung diseases in urban areas. So we will want to support some anti-pollution measures and research into cleaner energy.

Use of technology

The pervasive nature of technology in our lives, particularly that of mobile devices, has changed our society almost out of all recognition in the past ten years or so. Christians should join with other concerned people in seeking to address those areas in which this influence is most pernicious. For example, we should support campaigns for more safeguarding governance and for controls on online pornography in all its many forms, online gambling, cyberbullying, e-grooming, sexploitation,

AI-unconscious bias, and other discriminatory, immoral, or unethical abuses.

Preach about politics (without being partisan)

Pastors and leaders of Christian denominations need to consider the danger of causing divisions in the ranks if they express a political view that is clearly a matter of wisdom and judgment. There is a difference between what a church, represented by its leaders, says and what individual members do and say, speaking for themselves. If leaders make political statements, those who may disagree within their membership may be disaffected and it will be harder to pastor such people.

However, I also strongly suggest that, despite the associated risks, pastors and denominational or church network leaders should not shrink from commenting on politics. They can preach on political issues (such as immigration or economic policy) at the level of *principle*, and leave their hearers to work on the application to actual *policy*, which may in turn suggest which party may be supportive of those goals. If, however, there is a clear-cut Christian view on the topic (such as abortion or marriage) then it seems absolutely right for preachers to be clear on the application as well.

Be ready for opposition

It was spring 2012, and I was talking to the community liaison manager at a local housing association who had generously funded some of our church community work, including a café and youth activities. I had recently written a piece for the local free newspaper, saying I disagreed with the government's proposal to legalise gay marriage which said, '...whilst we respect the right of every individual to make their own life choices and do not support any unfair discrimination, we continue to believe that the nature of marriage, as it has always been defined, is the building block of community and is for the benefit of everyone in society, so we want to support the traditional, meaningful and everyday understanding of marriage – the voluntary union of one man and one woman for life, to the exclusion of all others.'

He told me that he was appalled by what I had written and that they would withdraw funding if I ever said anything like it again. I tried to point out that my opinion was legal, and more importantly, was a completely mainstream Christian view. This was a controversial proposed new law which sought to redefine marriage, and had many opponents.

This exchange was an early warning that on some issues, particularly those to do with personal identity and sexuality, very strong feelings are aroused when debating them. So as we engage in the political process, we need to be prepared to face vocal, and sometimes very angry, opposition from those who disagree with our views.

Governments in the West are generally predisposed to be positive about the social work done by the church but hostile to the moral and religious teachings of Christianity. (They are probably equally horrified by the moral teaching of most world religions but for a complex set of reasons they are less likely to say so.) Tim Farron, in the wake of his ousting from the leadership of the Liberal Democrats in 2017, famously said that he doesn't think that in the present day a Christian could ever be leader of a political party. I am not sure that is true and it hasn't been tested fully. In 2023 Kate Forbes came very close to being elected leader of the Scottish National Party but she probably lost because she was not the favoured candidate of her party leadership, not simply because she was an evangelical Christian. However, commenting on the intense criticism she received for expressing her views on sexuality and gender, Fraser Nelson writing in *The Daily Telegraph* said:

> Christians in politics have been accommodated through a policy of don't-ask, don't-tell. They learn how to disguise their faith and dodge tricky questions, believing no good can come of being seen to be religious. But it's getting harder now, in an era where people can lose their jobs for expressing the wrong sort of opinions.[18]
>
> There was also the recent case (March 2023) of a local councillor who was suspended after objecting to Pride flags being flown in her street.[19]

We shouldn't overreact to all this; Christians are not generally being harassed for their views on issues that are less divisive, and the degree of persecution can be overstated, but it would be naïve to imagine that political involvement of any sort is going to be a comfortable ride. In our world of instant communication and online thought-police, any opinion we give might escalate quickly into a highly emotional argument.

Freedom of speech and religion

I have left this topic to the end of the chapter because I do not think it should be our main priority and focus. I love the freedoms that we enjoy in this country to gather for worship, evangelise, and speak our minds. I support the right for all people to have these freedoms, even when they promote views with which I strongly disagree (such as other religions). It is part of the bedrock of a democratic nation that everyone should be able to express an opinion

---

18. https://www.telegraph.co.uk/news/2023/02/16/snp-has-rising-star-even-dangerous-union-sturgeon/ Accessed 16 February 2023.

19. https://www.dailymail.co.uk/news/article-11879693/Essex-Tory-Councillor-81-suspended-saying-doesnt-want-Pride-sex-flags-high-streets.html. Accessed 12 December 2023.

without fear of government oppression or intimidation by the mob.

So I think Christians should continue to oppose all legislation that seeks to limit such freedom. However, if in time we lose it, we should remember that many Christians throughout history have lived under persecuting rulers and still do so today. God's truth is never truly silenced and the church often grows more when under pressure than when it is at ease.

But it would be a great loss to the UK if the church's voice were to be 'cancelled'. We have a great legacy in this land of Christian history that has left its mark in all sorts of important ways. Christian teaching was highly influential in the shaping of our laws, our parliamentary system, our education, health and social services, and so much more. Christian belief has influenced our cultural values more than most people realise. This came about because people were willing to live faithfully for Christ in the secular realm, loving both God and their neighbour.

And as we do the same today, we will find that pretty much all our engagement with culture and community is political. It is my hope and prayer that, having read this book, you will be convinced of the need to get involved, and will have some ideas of how to go about it, for the glory of God.

Questions for reflection and discussion

1. Christians should not get involved in politics – do you agree or disagree?

2. How would you describe political participation by believers in the Bible?

3. How could you get involved, locally or nationally, to be an influence for good and a voice for God?

Conclusion

'Therefore, since we are surrounded by such a great cloud of witnesses, let us throw off everything that hinders and the sin that so easily entangles. And let us run with perseverance the race marked out for us, fixing our eyes on Jesus, the pioneer and perfecter of faith. For the joy that was set before him he endured the cross, scorning its shame, and sat down at the right hand of the throne of God. Consider him who endured such opposition from sinners, so that you will not grow weary and lose heart.'
(Hebrews 12:1-3)

Your marketplaces

So, you have made it to the end of this little book. You had to keep going through the boring bits, of which there were probably a few too many. But you persevered. Thank you!

You might at this point be feeling a bit overwhelmed. There were so many ideas and things to think about. Where to start? It's all a bit much. My only advice is, at the very least start somewhere, but start small. And then keep going. It's a race to run.

The burden of this book was to give some principles and practical ideas to help us move out into our marketplaces with the gospel and do our best for the 50 per cent of the population of the UK who don't (yet) know a practising Christian. We need to be well prepared for having conversations in private and in public. We don't

179

have all the answers, but we do have the truth to share and defend.

Maybe the way you might respond is to start going to the literal market squares near you for street preaching and street evangelism. Go into that marketplace to make disciples and teach them.

Some of you might venture into the mass media. I hope you have seen that it need not be as scary or as impossible as you might have once thought – and that there are real opportunities for more of us to have a voice for Christ. Go into that marketplace to make disciples and teach them.

Some of you might need to refocus the way you interact on the Internet. Rather than promoting yourself or your church, why not try to reshape your content so that you help people make friends with Jesus? Go into that marketplace to make disciples and teach them.

Others of you might be able to see a way to do Christian politics locally or nationally. Go into that marketplace to make disciples and teach them.

I trust in some way as God uses it, this book helps you to venture out to your marketplace.

Keep going, day after day

I also want to encourage you as the book comes to an end that we need to keep going. Paul had to visit the marketplace 'day after day', talking with whoever was there before he eventually saw fruit. We have to keep going. Keep praying. Keep working. Keep trying new things. Keep on reflecting and discussing how we reach more people with the gospel.

We have an endurance race to run. It won't be a quick fix. It's not a sprint – it's a marathon. It might at times be hard to keep going because we cannot see any fruit. We might face serious opposition. We might at times grow weary and lose heart. Sometimes our sin will hold us back. We might get distracted by problems in the church or other things in our lives and lose focus on the lost.

But keep going; keep moving out. Keep going because your eyes are fixed on Jesus. He perfects our race. He gives us joy as we witness His joy paving the way for us. And we keep running.

May God help us to keep going to our marketplace until faith gives way to sight, and we gather in the presence of the most excellent King of kings.

EDITED BY GRAHAM NICHOLLS

CHALLENGING

LEADERS

PREVENTING PASTORAL MALPRACTICE
AND INVESTIGATING ALLEGATIONS

Challenging Leaders

Preventing and Investigating Allegations of Pastoral Malpractice

edited by Graham Nicholls

ISBN: 978-1-5271-1028-1

A practical guide for church leaders looking to prevent, or navigate accusations of, pastoral malpractice.

Good spiritual leadership is vital to the health of a church. When leaders misuse their position and are controlling, egotistical and proud, they abuse the trust they have been given by the Lord. Abuse of power is not a new phenomenon, however, it is an ancient biblical category, and must be addressed.

There are delicate situations to be navigated. Drawing lines between abuse and normal, appropriate pastoral care, including warning, admonition and discipline is crucial, as is discovering when accusations are false.

The author team behind this book bring many years of pastoral experience, as well as wisdom and training in the area of abuse within the church.

Christian Focus Publications

Our mission statement –

STAYING FAITHFUL

In dependence upon God we seek to impact the world through literature faithful to His infallible Word, the Bible. Our aim is to ensure that the Lord Jesus Christ is presented as the only hope to obtain forgiveness of sin, live a useful life and look forward to heaven with Him.

Our books are published in four imprints:

CHRISTIAN FOCUS

Popular works including biographies, commentaries, basic doctrine and Christian living.

CHRISTIAN HERITAGE

Books representing some of the best material from the rich heritage of the church.

MENTOR

Books written at a level suitable for Bible College and seminary students, pastors, and other serious readers. The imprint includes commentaries, doctrinal studies, examination of current issues and church history.

CF4•K

Children's books for quality Bible teaching and for all age groups: Sunday school curriculum, puzzle and activity books; personal and family devotional titles, biographies and inspirational stories – because you are never too young to know Jesus!

Christian Focus Publications Ltd,
Geanies House, Fearn, Ross-shire,
IV20 1TW, Scotland, United Kingdom.
www.christianfocus.com